W9-COP-382

As consultant to the United States Senate Foreign Relations Committee, WILLIAM BADER is particularly concerned with the Middle East and South Asia, as well as disarmament and military questions. He has served as a Foreign Service Officer in the Department of State's Office of Atlantic Political-Military Affairs.

Mr. Bader holds a doctorate in history from Princeton University and was a lecturer in its history department and a Research Associate at the Princeton Center of International Studies in 1964–1965. He is the author of *Austria Between East and West: 1945–1955.*

The United States and the Spread of Nuclear Weapons

by
WILLIAM B. BADER

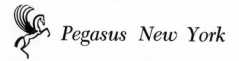 Pegasus New York

To Gretta

PUBLISHED FOR
THE CENTER OF INTERNATIONAL STUDIES
PRINCETON UNIVERSITY

ACKNOWLEDGMENTS   This book was written under the sponsorship of the Center of International Studies, Princeton University. I am deeply indebted to the Center's director, Klaus Knorr, whose patience, good humor, and valuable advice stood me well during the preparation of the volume.

In the writing of this book I have benefited from the expert advice of many colleagues at the Center of International Studies. Thornton Read, Oran Young, and Richard Falk have all read the several drafts of the manuscript and have made many helpful suggestions.

A portion of this book has appeared in *Foreign Affairs*. I am especially grateful to the editors, Hamilton Fish Armstrong and Philip W. Quigg, for their skill and assistance.

Lest there be some misunderstanding, I want to make it clear that no inferences should be drawn from anything in this book as to the opinions of the Senate Foreign Relations Committee or any member thereof. This study was drafted before I came to the Committee and, except for up-dating, remains essentially the same in its approach and conclusions. I am solely and fully responsible for the contents of this volume.

Table of Contents

Introduction

For a man with an admirable sense of proportion and dispassion in coming to terms with pressing problems, John F. Kennedy's public statements on the spread of nuclear weapons to additional countries had a faint air of despair about them. Every man has his private nightmare, and President Kennedy's nightmare seems to have been the possibility, as he put it in March of 1963, that in the 1970's the President of the United States would be forced to face a world "in which 15 or 20 or 25 nations may have these weapons," a situation which he regarded "as the greatest possible danger and hazard." [1] Kennedy's sense of urgency when it came to the proliferation problem was made quite explicit during his report to the nation on the nuclear test ban treaty:

> We have a great obligation—all four nuclear powers [China had not yet detonated its first device] have a great obligation—*to use whatever time remains* to prevent the spread of nuclear weapons, to persuade other countries not to test, transfer, acquire, possess, or produce such weapons. [2]

If President Kennedy seemed possessed with an apocalyptic vision of a world abounding with harebrained or malevolent nuclear powers, Secretary of Defense McNamara has been no more comforting—or specific—on one of the most crucial issues of our time. In October of 1964, after predicting that the costs of developing a usable nuclear weapon will go down dramatically as the technology becomes simpler, Mr. McNamara drew a painfully bleak picture of the future:

> You can imagine the danger that the world would face if 10, 20, or 30 nations possessed nuclear weapons instead of the four that possess them today. . . . The danger to other nations increases geometrically with the increase in the number of nations possessing these warheads,

and therefore, it is the policy of our Government to act to deter the diffusion, [the] proliferation of nuclear weapons.[3]

In response to the threat of a further spread of nuclear arms, the United States government has adopted a policy of unswerving hostility to all forms of proliferation, a policy which has taken on all the trappings of dogma. In considering this "dogma," most Americans would agree that it is hardly arguable that any increase in the number of nuclear nations is a bad thing. We have grown accustomed to the demands, and certainties, of a bipolar world with the United States and the Soviet Union controlling the pace and pattern of crisis involving nuclear weapons. Any new center of nuclear power, whatever its form, represents an intrusion, and potentially a threat to involve the United States in a nuclear war not of its choosing. But once this is said, we are left with the fact that no amount of painful disapproval, dark and foreboding warnings, or even the erection of technological barriers, seems to have dissuaded those countries bent on acquiring a nuclear capability.

One of the difficulties in adjusting to the thought of a world resplendent with all shades and varieties of new nuclear "powers" is that when the imagination evoked by Mr. McNamara actually begins to catalogue the potential horrors of such a world—accidental or unauthorized use of such weapons, nuclear blackmail, the possibility that a third country could provoke a nuclear conflict between the larger powers—it becomes difficult to get beyond the worst possible consequences of proliferation. It is small wonder, then, that "nuclear proliferation" has joined government waste and regional poverty as something that every responsible American leader is against.

In their apparent preoccupation with the mathematics of proliferation, however, many United States officials seem to have taken for granted that, with regard to nuclear weapons, the national experience of one country is relevant to others. But is the French experience with nuclear weapons relevant to our understanding of West Germany's nuclear problems; is the Indian dilemma over a national nuclear weapons program germane to anticipating how Japan will behave in the nuclear field? Will national attitudes change if a non-proliferation pact becomes a reality? On another plane, is a policy of unrelenting opposition to all forms of the spread of nuclear weapons sensible? Are all forms of nuclear proliferation equally bad? Is the acquisition of nuclear weapons by, say, Sweden, really as bad as by a country such as the United Arab Republic? Such questions are important because an attempt at supplying answers will, I believe, illustrate the liabilities of dealing with the spread of nuclear arms on the abstract level of the "Nth country problem."

Most studies on the subject of proliferation with which I am familiar have centered on an analysis of the diminishing technological barriers to acquiring nuclear weapons, citing the countries closest to developing the necessary skills,[4] and discussing the motivations for opting for such weapons primarily in terms of the experience Britain and France have had.[5] In the chapters that follow an attempt is made to move the discussion of nuclear proliferation away from the "numbers game"—speculating on how many countries "could have" nuclear weapons by "such and such time." Instead, the emphasis is shifted to a history of the United States' changing attitudes and policies toward nuclear proliferation. In contrasting these attitudes toward the spread of nuclear weapons with the national circumstances of some of the important non-nuclear states, the object will be to begin to test the proposition that international or universal solutions—such as a non-proliferation treaty—are actually responsive to the problem of the spread of nuclear arms.

I

The United States and the Nuclear Dilemma "In the Manner of Making War"

> . . . The progress of science, of chemistry in particular, is such that things quite incredible yesterday are realities today. We can foresee the use of projectiles, or other things filled with deleterious gas and soporifics, which, hurled down from balloons into the midst of troops, would disable them at once. Since such attacks cannot be guarded against, they resemble treachery; and all that resembles treachery should be scrupulously eliminated. Let us be chivalrous even in the manner of making war!—*Gen. den Beer Poortugael, delegate of the Netherlands to the First Hague Peace Conference, May 29, 1899.*

M. Couve de Murville's fine Gallic touch for needling the United States has rarely been more effective than in a speech before the French National Assembly in November of 1964 when he went right to the heart of the United States' nuclear dilemma. The French Foreign Minister's attack on the logic of the United States' "non-dissemination" policy was brief, and pointed:

> How can one claim to deny to others, unless they voluntarily renounce it for themselves, what one permits oneself? Experience proves, moreover, that this is never accomplished, except through force, which has never to my knowledge been considered. The solution, the only solu-

tion, is the total destruction of the existing arsenals and the banning of all new manufacture, both under effective control.[1]

For all the patent weaknesses in de Murville's "solution," this brief paragraph exposes the painful paradox of America's present position on nuclear proliferation; and poses the question of the relative merits of two sharply contrasting methods of slowing the spread of nuclear weapons. His second point which raises the question of the practicality of retarding the spread of nuclear weapons by banning the weapons and destroying existing arsenals will not be dealt with here. But de Murville's first point poses an important issue of record—that is, how the United States found itself in a position of denying to others "what one permits oneself," and what this policy of denial implies for the success of our non-proliferation efforts. What follows is not intended to be a complete historical study of the development of United States policy toward the spread of nuclear weapons during the period of atomic monopoly, but an attempt to identify some of the characteristics of that policy that persist today.

Underlying all discussion within the United States on the proliferation issue is a very basic question which for many remains disturbingly unresolved: Are nuclear weapons merely one more revolutionary weapon to be absorbed into our pattern of international relations, or are these weapons something akin to poison gases that have somehow escaped the censure of being internationally outlawed as a legitimate weapon?[2] The question is important not because it demands an answer—the answer was given over Hiroshima and Nagasaki—but because the consequences of this answer have placed the United States at a psychological disadvantage in coping with the spread of nuclear weapons. It is difficult to be convincing on the horrors of nuclear war and the inadvisability of opting for nuclear weapons when the United States has used them in the past and is relying on such weapons as the backbone of the American defense system.

Even after Hiroshima the United States conceivably could have pressed for an international agreement placing atomic bombs in a category of illegitimate weapons. Such an international prohibition is not without precedent. For example, at the First Hague Peace Conference in 1899 the major European powers agreed to outlaw poison gas and dumdum bullets as legitimate weapons of war.[3] But here the objection can be raised that Imperial Germany violated the prohibition in 1915, as did the Italians in 1935 against the Ethiopians. Nevertheless, in both cases, Germany and Italy admitted that they had strayed outside the bounds of internationally acceptable warfare, offering only the excuse that their enemies had used the gas first, as was Germany's explanation, or that the victims were outside the protection of international agreements, as was Mussolini's crude and unconvincing argument.

The major point of this experience with the outlawing of toxic gases is not that it was twice broken, but that the violators were severely censured internationally, and the prohibition was re-enforced and strengthened as a result of this censure. This prohibition remains today, much to the chagrin of many who argue that the proper selection and use of biological and chemical agents in certain circumstances is both more humane and efficient than conventional or nuclear force. The champions of the selective use of such agents argue that toxic weapons are an integral part of modern war and complain that the United States government has unwisely persisted in emphasizing the "mysterious" and "sinister" nature of chemical and biological warfare.[4] Despite these protestations, there is no reason to believe that the United States will modify the *de facto* "no first use" policy on the use of toxic weapons established in 1942 in warning Hitler not to use them first.

But what of nuclear weapons in this context? Clearly it would have been difficult for the United States to have taken the initiative in outlawing nuclear weapons. Once the weapons had been used such a policy would have represented to many a repudiation of the decision to bomb the Japanese cities. It is interesting to speculate, however, on what would have happened if the United States had offered to renounce the use of nuclear weapons in 1945 if an international covenant outlawing the use of such weapons could have been agreed upon.

Alternately, in the years after 1945 the United States could have taken a very hard line on the use of nuclear weapons, similar to the one taken by the then Captain A. T. Mahan at the Hague Conference. Responding to a proposal forbidding the employment of lethal gases, Mahan contended that the objections to gas as "barbarous" were the same charges leveled against firearms in the Middle Ages, later on against mortars, and more recently torpedoes—all of which were eventually adopted by all those who could afford them. Moreover, Mahan stated that while he represented a country that was as humane as the next, he also represented a country which might have to wage war and thus had no intention of depriving itself of a useful means of waging such a war. In the opinion of Mahan's government, "from a humane standpoint it is no more cruel to asphyxiate one's enemies by means of deleterious gases than with water, that is to say, by drowning them, as happens when a vessel is sunk by a torpedo of a torpedo-boat."[5] Despite Mahan's protests, the resolution against the use of gases was adopted, with the United States the only nation voting against it.

In Mahan's comparison, the substitution of death by nuclear fire for "asphyxiation . . . by deleterious gases" and death from a Hamburg or Tokyo fire raid for death "by drowning" comes readily to mind. But United States officials in 1945, impressed with the enormity of nuclear power as a military weapon, chose to avoid this line of justification for considering the use of nuclear weapons as a legitimate means of waging war. Instead we chose a line that defied all that was known about the history of military technology. We chose to believe that our technological lead in the nuclear weapons field was so immense and the process itself so complicated and expensive that the United States could rely on employing those weapons as the substance of its world military power while simultaneously remaining certain that none but the strongest of competitors could duplicate our accomplishment.

Representative of the United States' initial approach was the devising of an international control system over the world supplies of fissionable materials. Originating in 1946 as the Acheson-Lilienthal Report, and later modified into the so-called Baruch Plan, this program envisioned the creation of an International Atomic Development Authority under the United Nations which, in addition to control of the world's nuclear raw materials, would have managerial control of all atomic energy activities considered potentially dangerous to world peace, as well as the power to inspect and license all other atomic installations.[6] Although the Baruch Plan died a-borning when the Soviet Union refused to consider it, the offer itself, which was truly revolutionary in the effect it would have had on national sovereignty, now enjoys an exalted place in the hagiography of American disarmament tracts and speeches. No American statement on disarmament and the dangers of proliferation seems complete without a reference to what might have been "if only" the Soviets had accepted the Baruch Plan.

The truth of the matter seems to be that the Baruch Plan, while a generous gesture, could be interpreted, and was so interpreted by the Soviets, as an attempt to play out the United States atomic monopoly as long as possible. In any eulogy of the Baruch Plan heard today in the United States, scant attention is given to the fact that the United States promised to cease the manufacture of atomic weapons only after an acceptable system of control and punishment of offenders was in effective operation. In other words, first the negotiations over control and inspection, then talk about the banning of nuclear weapons. In the meantime, the United States would proceed with enlarging and refining its atomic arsenal. For the Soviets to have accepted such a plan would have contributed to their problem of duplicating the American bomb. As long as the United States had a monopoly on atomic weapons and intended to use them if circumstances so demanded, the Soviet Union had no real choice but to reject a proposal which might interfere with their efforts to develop a nuclear counter to the American advantage.

The rationale behind the American decision to defend the use of nuclear weapons as a legitimate form of warfare while simultaneously denying the right of the "less responsible" countries, be they ally or enemy, to follow our example, is well rooted both in the circumstances in which the United States found itself immediately after the war and in our early estimates of the timetable of the challenge to America's nuclear monopoly. These circumstances and assumptions include:

(1) Whatever misgivings the United States may have had as to the ethics and military soundness of relying on nuclear weapons as the backbone of our defense system, the possession of these weapons allowed us to retain our great power status after the war without supporting the large conventional force maintained by the Soviet Union. Whatever logistic difficulties President Truman had in getting

the troops home by Christmas of 1945 were not a patch on the political difficulties he would have had had he not brought them home.

(2) Imperial Germany used toxic gases in 1915 as the United States used nuclear weapons in 1945; the first case was a clear violation of the international ethics of warfare; the second case clearly could have been so characterized. What made the German case so blatantly an illegitimate manner of waging war was not just that Germany had signed an international covenant to that effect, but that Germany lost the war. The paradox was that the western Allies, who had mounted an intensive anti-gas campaign in order to counter the German superiority in this field, soon became the prisoners of their own propaganda. The situation was profoundly different in 1945. The Allies won the war and the United States the right to define the future of nuclear weapons. We chose to define them as an awesome, terrifyingly revolutionary, but legitimate means of waging war for some nations.

(3) The fairly widespread assumption made in the West during the first years of the Cold War that the United States' atomic monopoly would, as long as it lasted, improve our bargaining position with the Soviet Union. Winston Churchill, who should have known better at least after the Czechoslovakian coup, put the argument this way in October of 1948:

> We ought not to go jogging along improvident, incompetent, waiting for something to turn up. The Western Nations will be far more likely to reach a lasting settlement, without bloodshed, if they formulate their just demands while they have the atomic power and before the Russian Communists have got it too.[7]

(4) Perhaps the most fragile piece of assumptive scaffolding supporting America's early policies with regard to the spread of nuclear weapons was the reverence with which we viewed our own handiwork in developing the bomb. The working assumption in 1945 among most experts was that the United States had considerable time to exploit its atomic monopoly. This view was typified by a man who had every reason to know, Major General Leslie R. Groves, the Director of the Manhattan Project. It was General Groves' view in 1945 that it would take other nations, including Russia, many years to match our success. The reason he gave for this was not the lack

of knowledge or scientific competence, but that others did not have the engineering talent or facilities.

This assumption that a significant engineering and technological gap existed between the United States and the rest of the world was dramatically and conclusively underscored by the report of a committee assembled by Secretary of War Stimson in 1945. The committee consisted of officials and engineers from the industries involved in the production of atomic weapons, and an impressive array of scientists, including Enrico Fermi, J. Robert Oppenheimer, and Ernest Lawrence. It was the estimate of this group that it would probably take the Soviet Union ten years—that is, until late 1955—to produce an atomic bomb.[8]

It is, of course, not quite clear how this estimate was made but the detonation by the Soviet Union of a nuclear device in 1949 pointedly demonstrated that the United States had over-estimated the difficulties the Russians would encounter in constructing a bomb. The estimate was probably the result of a combination of a too rigid application of American standards of engineering, a tendency to think of the process as prohibitively expensive (the United States spent some $2.2 billion in developing the first bomb and has invested about $33 billion in its Atomic Energy program since 1940), all topped off with a dash of ethnic smugness.[9] Less understandable has been the persistence of this tendency to downgrade the capabilities of other nations in the nuclear weapons field.[10]

Given the above background, it is little wonder that the United States found it imperative to guard our nuclear secrets closely, and, at least in some circles, to regard the success of others in the nuclear field as the result of traitorous acts on the part of Americans.[11] Fortunately we are now coming to realize that there are inexorable laws governing the flow of scientific information. Nuclear technology is like any other scientific skill; it soon becomes the hallmark of a modern society. And as this skill finds its inevitable place in industrializing and modernizing societies, the monopoly of the innovators is gradually eroded in the same way that Great Britain gradually lost her industrial advantage over the continent as the nineteenth century wore on.

This process of technological leveling in the nuclear weapons field has been accelerated—and complicated—by the vast potential of atomic energy for peaceful uses. In his remarks before the Third United Nations International Conference on the Peaceful Uses of Atomic Energy, Dr. Glenn T. Seaborg, Chairman of the United States Atomic Energy Commission, marveled that "so much had been accomplished in only twenty years." In Dr. Seaborg's view, the world has now moved in the short years since the discovery in the late nineteen-thirties of the process of nuclear fission to a point where nuclear energy has become an economic fuel source "in limited but important areas."[12] Dr. Seaborg went on to report that "the installed nuclear capacity of the world has increased from 1955, with only five megawatts, to 1958 and 185 megawatts. Today, in 1964, we have about 5,000 megawatts. The future prognosis is also excellent. One can see that by 1970 the total world capacity will be about 25,000 megawatts and by 1980 this will have increased to 150,000 to 250,000 megawatts."[13] Moreover, it appears that entry into the nuclear energy field is becoming profitable as well as prestigious. Buoyed by the prospect that nuclear energy is becoming a commercial reality, that it now seems possible to extract uranium from seawater at acceptable costs, and that reactors may hold the answer to desalinization of water, the nuclear energy field holds increasing interest for private industry. Commercial interests with advanced merchandising techniques and competitive bidding have entered the nuclear fields.[14] Under these conditions, it is hardly debatable that the rate at which nuclear materials, technology, and information will be distributed, already rapid, is bound to accelerate. The implications of such a world-wide surge in interest in nuclear energy for the probable pace of nuclear weapons proliferation are enormous.

Considering the fact that the nuclear mechanics of a peaceful or a weapons program are, in certain circumstances, virtually indistinguishable up until the last stages,[15] the scrupulous and all too self-conscious way in which the participants in United Nations conferences on the peaceful uses of atomic energy ignore the prodigal son of nuclear physics is most ironic. The fact is that the official papers and proceedings of these conferences (held in 1955, 1958, and 1964) join the official history of the Los Alamos project—the so-called Smyth Report—and various technical journals as prime public sources of information on how to build an atomic bomb. The magnitude and completeness of this public information has increased to a point where Arnold Kramish, an expert on these matters, is forced to conclude in a dazzling metaphor that "the genie has been handed to other nations on a plutonium platter." [16]

In the spring of 1966 the United States Senate adopted unanimously a resolution offered by Senator Pastore which commended President Johnson's "serious and urgent efforts to negotiate international agreements limiting the spread of nuclear weapons." In a letter of appreciation to Senator Pastore, the President, who has called nuclear proliferation the "gravest of all unresolved human issues," wrote that ". . . this resolution would reinforce our urgent pursuit of a treaty to prevent the spread of nuclear weapons." [17]

Such high resolve and a compelling sense of urgency, now so characteristic of United States efforts to achieve a non-proliferation treaty, is, surprisingly enough, of very recent origin. It has only been since 1961 that United States disarmament proposals have included provisions calling for a ban on the further spread of nuclear weapons; and only since 1958 has the United States categorically opposed increases in the number of states possessing nuclear weapons. Moreover, it was not until 1965 that the United States began actively to seek a non-proliferation agreement. And one need only recall the abuse Adlai Stevenson was subjected to during the 1956 election campaign to appreciate how grudgingly the United States came to the conclusion that a partial test ban could be in our interest. The reasons for this shift in the United States attitude toward a formal test ban and a non-proliferation agreement are worth considering, for they provide a useful background to the genesis of the troublesome ambiguity now plaguing the United States policy toward the spread of nuclear weapons.

To say that the United States was slow in pressing for a non-proliferation treaty and a limited test ban treaty is not to suggest that during the Eisenhower administration, and the first years of the Democratic administration, there was a lack of concern about the spread of nuclear weapons. The difference was one of emphasis and priority. The emphasis during the Eisenhower period was on the international control on the fissionable materials that could be used for weapons. Gaining control over fissionable materials was considered an adequate stop-gap measure while the United States and the

Soviet Union negotiated the kind of comprehensive disarmament system that would bring all national armaments under international control and inspection. The nature of this recurrent theme in United States disarmament efforts during the 1950's is best expressed in a United Nations General Assembly resolution (from which the Soviet bloc abstained) adopted in November of 1953. This resolution, sponsored by the United States, called for ". . . the effective international control of atomic energy to ensure the prohibition of atomic weapons and the use of atomic energy for peaceful purposes only." [18]

This belief that the international control of fissionable materials could be "effective" in checking the spread of nuclear weapons until a general disarmament agreement was achieved was the centerpiece of American nuclear policy during the 1950's. We now know how faulty the assumption was that international control of nuclear materials would be enough to check the spread of nuclear weapons; what we cannot know is what might have been accomplished if the United States had had this illusion stripped away in the early 1950's rather than some ten years later.

Illustrative of the American attitude toward the spread of nuclear weapons during the 1950's is an excerpt from a statement made by Henry Cabot Lodge to the United Nations Disarmament Commission on July 3, 1956: "For our part, while we offer to work for control and limitations of atomic weapons, we believe that their elimination is impractical because we know . . . that there is no way to verify by any presently known scientific means of inspection that they have in fact been eliminated, . . . nor will we make any commitment which will prevent their use in the defense of democratic nations against assault by armies with vast reserves of disciplined manpower at the command of powers which would themselves be able, at any time, to turn to the use of atomic weapons." [19]

Thus, Mr. Lodge at least partially developed one of the major themes of American nuclear weapons policy in the 1950's; American security interests would not be properly served by partial disarmament measures and particularly such partial steps as a test ban moratorium should not be agreed to except in the context of a comprehensive and safeguarded (fully verified) disarmament agreement.

Another important theme of American nuclear policy in the 1950's was our determination to maintain complete flexibility in the use and deployment of our nuclear weapons. This determination was reinforced by our estimate that the developing nuclear weapons program of the United States and that of our allies would be crippled by a partial test ban or a non-proliferation agreement. The United States record in the 1950's on a nuclear test ban and our attempts to achieve a non-proliferation agreement may help to show this.

Agitation for a nuclear test ban first found both a respectable and persuasive voice in 1954 when Indian Prime Minister Nehru, responding in part to worldwide concern over the injury to Japanese fishermen after an American test, proposed a "standstill agreement." As Nehru explained, such an agreement on the cessation of testing was imperative "even if arrangements about the discontinuance of production and stockpiling must await more substantial agreements among those principally concerned."[20]

In late June of 1954, however, the United States frankly admitted that the time was not right for a test ban moratorium and we would, therefore, be forced to reject all such proposals on testing unless such a test ban came as part of a comprehensive disarmament agreement. President Eisenhower made this position clear in February, 1955, when in response to a question on the desirability of a test ban he stated at a press conference that the United States saw nothing "to be gained by pretending to take little bits of items and deal with them separately." Such a ban would have to come in the context of a "decent and proper disarmament proposal."[21] Again in October of 1956, in response to a Soviet proposal to stop testing, President Eisenhower replied that "we must continue—until a properly safeguarded international agreement can be reached—to develop our strength in the most advanced weapons—for the sake of our own national safety, for the sake of all free nations, for the sake of peace itself." As for the health hazards of testing, the President gave an explanation of possible use to today's French and Communist Chinese press offices: "The continuance of the present rate of H-bomb testing—by the most sober and responsible scientific judgment—does not imperil the health of humanity."[22]

This United States position of resisting a suspension of nuclear testing was to last until 1958, when the United States dropped its insistence on coupling a test ban with a larger disarmament program.

What remained, however, was Washington's determination that any test ban would require an adequate verification system.

The reasons for the United States' hesitant, and often intractable, position on disarmament and arms controls proposals during the 1950's can be found in Washington appraisal of the strategic balance. In the 1950's the United States felt that its own security interests required the continued testing of our own weapons and the concurrent development of a British thermonuclear weapons program. We also felt that it was of greater importance to maintain maximum flexibility with regard to the transfer and deployment of our own nuclear weapons than it was to check the spread of nuclear weapons. Indeed, it can certainly be said of the Eisenhower Administration that it placed a higher premium on nuclear weapons cooperation with our allies—even at the price of encouraging and stimulating independent atomic weapons programs—than it did on seeking international agreements retarding the spread of atomic weapons. This was not entirely due to the Eisenhower Administration's sense of priorities. It was also partially the result of a misplaced confidence in the effectiveness of the "atoms for peace" approach. Nevertheless, the major objective of the Eisenhower Administration was to offset what we considered the initial strategic advantage gained by the Soviet Union in 1957 with Sputnik. This anxiety over the Sputnik achievement was compounded by the still secret Gaither Report which apparently contended that the United States was at a dangerous military disadvantage vis-a-vis the Soviet Union. Responding to this threat, President Eisenhower, who was also determined to avoid a major increase in the budget, suggested that the talents and energies of the Allies be used in offsetting the Soviet threat. Consequently, the President asked Congress in January of 1958 for a major revision to the Atomic Energy legislation to permit a greater degree of nuclear cooperation with our Allies.

Certainly the most revealing remarks on the American international attitude toward the nuclear weapons question in the 1950's, particularly immediately after Sputnik, were those made by Secretary Dulles in May of 1958 at a secret briefing of the American Chiefs of Mission in Europe. In commenting on the fact that the Soviet Union in March, 1958, had declared an indefinite suspension of its own nuclear weapons tests, Dulles said:

We had an important meeting in Washington prior to the suspension of testing by the Soviet Union regarding the possibility of our announcing the end of our testing after completion of the present series, and getting out our announcement before they issued theirs. This would have been a tremendous propaganda coup and would have certainly upset the Communists. I think I can say the decisive reason why that was not done was not a United States consideration, but the feeling that some of our allies would feel that we had done them dirt had we done that, so we did not do it.

[As to the future], a great deal depends upon amending the Atomic Energy Act and we are trying to amend it in the fashion to permit us to share with our allies under certain conditions the benefit of our knowledge and testing to date. Under these conditions the UK for example might be willing to agree to a test suspension.

Dulles felt all of this had been quite "awkward" because

. . . the general attitude of Congress is that while they are willing to have such an exchange of information with the UK, they do not want to have it with France or any other countries.[23]

Dulles thus summed up the White House's position on the nuclear question as of the late 1950's: the priorities of our own testing program, deference to the sensitivities of Great Britain which had not yet completed its own testing series, and finally plans for sharing our nuclear knowledge and weapons with our allies with hope of offsetting the Soviet advantage brought on by Sputnik. It should be noted here, as elsewhere in the record of the 1950's, that non-proliferation was not considered a problem of great magnitude, at least not a problem requiring self-restrictions on our own plans for sharing our atomic plenty with our allies.

From his own experience as NATO's Supreme Allied Commander Europe (SACEUR), President Eisenhower was certainly aware of the problem he would have in convincing Congress that the United States should share its nuclear secrets with our NATO allies. Mr. Eisenhower has recently written of his exasperation when he was NATO's commander with the McMahon Act and the barrier this legislation created against cooperation with our NATO allies:

The matter of nuclear strength and possible deployment was troublesome from the beginning. . . . The law, as written, ignored certain prior agreements on these subjects reached by Mr. Churchill and President Roosevelt at Quebec and later by President Truman and Prime Minister Atlee. Moreover, it was written on the assumption that the United States had—and probably could retain—a monopoly in the nuclear science. In 1951 the law prevented us from making any workable agreements with our partners in NATO respecting nuclear weapons—indeed it was difficult and embarrassing, because of the restrictions imposed on us, even to discuss the matter intelligently and thoroughly.[24]

The responsibility for this policy of denying design data, information on weapons effects, and atomic materials to our Allies is a matter of dispute. Former President Eisenhower, at least by implication, suggests it was the fault of Congress that the United States has been so slow to bring our atomic energy legislation in line with the nuclear "facts of life." Congressional sources, however, contend that President Eisenhower had many opportunities to request significant modifications of the atomic energy legislation but failed to push hard enough or give convincing reasons why the laws should be changed. My own reading of the public testimony on the various modifications of the McMahon Act—1951, 1955, 1958, and 1964—suggests that the Joint Committee on Atomic Energy and the AEC have been considerably more conservative and skeptical over extending the areas of atomic cooperation than the White House.

The history of various pieces of legislation dealing with atomic energy information, beginning with the Atomic Energy Act of 1946, is a revealing index of the United States uncertainty in relating this terrifying new category of power to the demands of an alliance system. The original Atomic Energy Act of 1946, particularly as amended in 1951, prohibited the release of sensitive data on the design of atomic weapons and the transfer of fissionable materials to ally and non-ally alike. The intent of this legislation reflected our confidence at that time in the effectiveness of total security as a barrier to those who would duplicate our efforts and in an ability to counter the Soviet nuclear menace alone. In 1955, however, Congress, now aware of the diminishing effectiveness of total nuclear security and concerned about the effectiveness of NATO in the face of the Soviet nuclear threat, amended the Atomic Energy Act. This amendment permitted the transfer to NATO countries of information on nuclear defense plans, on the external characteristics of nuclear weapons, and on the training of NATO personnel in the employment of US atomic weapons.

In 1958, in response to President Eisenhower's request, the Atomic Energy Act was again overhauled. The 1958 amendments (Public Law 479 of July 2, 1958) authorized under certain specific conditions the transfer to our allies of: (1) the non-nuclear parts of atomic weapons; (2) fissionable nuclear materials suitable for the development of, or use in, nuclear weapons; (3) sensitive information concerning nuclear weapons; and (4) nuclear equipment such as military reactors.[25] As already mentioned, the rationale behind this radical departure from past policies had its roots largely in the dramatic impact that the launching of Sputnik I and II in the fall of 1957 had on official Washington. In his State of the Union message of January 8, 1958, President Eisenhower expressed the need the White House felt for the United States to cooperate with its allies in hopes of closing as rapidly as possible the technological gap Russia presumably had opened with the Sputnik performance. It is revealing, if not slightly embarrassing, in the light of our present effort to hinder and harass the French nuclear effort, to recall Eisenhower's words to Congress less than ten years ago:

> It is wasteful in the extreme for friendly allies to consume talent and money in solving problems that their friends have already solved—all because of artificial barriers to sharing. We cannot afford to cut ourselves off from the brilliant talents and minds of scientists in friendly countries. The task ahead will be hard enough without handcuffs of our own making.[26]

President Eisenhower's declaration in favor of cooperating with "friendly countries" notwithstanding, we soon forged for ourselves a sturdy pair of those very handcuffs. First of all, the 1958 amendments were carefully designed not to encourage additional countries to enter the nuclear weapons field. As the forwarding letter of the AEC when submitting the proposed legislation to the Congress put it:

> It is not intended that manufactured components of weapons could be transferred under this amendment, nor that we promote the entry of additional countries into the field of production of nuclear weapons.[27]

In order to make it clear that the United States was dead set against facilitating the entry of new nuclear powers into the field, the final version of the legislation specified that the transfer of atomic secrets and materials under this law was restricted to those nations who have already made *"substantial progress* in the development of atomic weapons. . . ."[28] Moreover, such arrangements as made under the provisions of the law must "not constitute an unreasonable risk to common defense and security."[29]

As to which countries were deemed eligible under these exacting standards, the Joint Committee on Atomic Energy was straightforward enough in reporting the bill out to Congress—"only Great Britain meets the standards."[30] And here we come right to the heart of the matter of nuclear sharing. Despite President Eisenhower's use of the plural in calling for cooperation with "friendly countries," the intention of the legislation was not to provide guidelines for sharing nuclear weapons resources with Allies but to bring Great Britain, and only Great Britain, into a special nuclear relationship with the United States. Mr. Harold S. Vance, a Commissioner of the Atomic Energy Commission, was perhaps most candid about this discriminatory policy before the Joint Committee:

> Now our dilemma is this: We admit, to ourselves, that we want to discriminate among our allies, but we cannot admit it to them. Now the way to handle this situation is for you gentlemen [the Joint Committee] to write some criteria into this law that we can use as a basis for our refusal to treat all of our allies alike.[31]

When confronted with questions as to how the administration was going to finesse such discriminatory legislation with allies such as France or Australia, its champions were vague and allusive in the first case and unconcerned in the second.[32] For example, during the 1958 hearing on the proposed amendments, the then Secretary of State, John Foster Dulles, was asked what he thought of the likelihood that any of the SEATO (South East Asia Treaty Organization) nations could ever qualify under the act. Dulles' reply is an excellent example of the persistence of the idea that the development of a nuclear weapons program was a formidable task, even for a nation with a substantial industrial base. The dialogue went as follows:

> *Senator (Clinton P.) Anderson.* What do you think is the likelihood of the extension of nuclear weapons material and secrets to any of the SEATO nations, say Australia?
>
> *Secretary Dulles.* I think that it is practically so unlikely that it could be regarded as almost an impossibility, because they do not have the financial resources to develop themselves into a nation which would qualify.
>
> *Senator Anderson.* Are you sure the Australians are not pretty close to a weapon right now?
>
> *Secretary Dulles.* I think they are close to having the necessary technical knowledge, but to move from the technical knowledge to the making and testing of an instrument to be sure that it will go off, that is a very big gap indeed.[33]

Admittedly, the American policy toward the spread of nuclear weapons technology is not entirely negative, merely selective. While the fact that the United States is contributing to the nuclear weapons program of at least one other country and has legislation on the books that ostensibly rewards those who show "substantial progress in the development of atomic weapons" cannot be denied, any suggestion that such policies contribute to the proliferation problem is categorically denied by American officials. This denial rests on two arguments:

(1) The provisions of the Atomic Energy Act amendments apply only to those countries which already have made "substantial progress in the development of atomic weapons"—"substantial progress" being defined by Secretary of State Dulles as applying only ". . . in the case of the countries or the country which already has nuclear capacity."[34] Therefore, the argument runs, such transfers as do occur will not contribute to the proliferation problem.

(2) Rather than acting as a stimulus to the spread of nuclear weapons, the amendments will act to brake the pace of proliferation. In the light of what we know about the complexities and sensitivities involved when it comes to handling command and control problems with our allies, Mr. Dulles' description of how the amendments would slow the spread of weapons is a revealing one indeed:

> I believe this program taken as a whole is going to be acceptable to those allies who presently have a potentiality themselves of developing

nuclear weapons and they will not go into the expensive business that would be involved in trying to develop for themselves an independent nuclear capacity. That is what we want to check. This is an intermediate course which gives them sufficient benefit out of our nuclear capacity so that the incentive to become an independent nuclear power, in our opinion, will very largely disappear. *I do think that the danger is not that this legislation will promote fourth power countries. I think on the contrary if we do not get this legislation that will be a stimulus for them to go out and do it on their own.*[35]

The first argument possesses a certain validity if it is agreed, first, that once a nation has attained nuclear weapons status it will never give it up by renouncing its nuclear weapons or, less dramatically, allowing the force to degenerate, and, secondly, that an established nuclear country enjoying the atomic largess of the United States will not in turn help a "fourth" country. The first point is, for the first time, being tested in Britain where the Labour government is plagued by doubts over the genuine independence of the British force. The second may also be tested in Europe where Britain's nuclear skills, long rejuvenated by American exchanges, may yet be Britain's ticket of admission to any future Western European military community.

There is another flaw in the argument that because the transfer of atomic military information and materials provided for in our atomic energy legislation is restricted to countries which have already made "substantial" progress in weapons development such arrangements do not contribute to the spread of nuclear weapons. The question is whether the vague criteria given for substantial progress will not encourage a country considering a weapons program to press ahead in hopes of eventually attaining the "special" nuclear relationship enjoyed by Britain. And could we refuse, given the laws already on the books? What about West Germany, or India, if the latter should sign a mutual defense agreement with the United States and thus technically become eligible under the law?

Even the use of the term "substantial progress" may come back to haunt the United States as the capacity to make such progress becomes increasingly widespread. The 1958 legislation itself does not define "substantial progress," leaving the criteria to the discretion of the executive branch with all the implications this carte blanche has for the future of the proliferation problem.[36] For its part, the Joint Committee on Atomic Energy included a definition of "substantial progress" in its report to the Congress. It was admitted in this report that the application of this definition, which does not appear in the legislation, rests on the "good faith" of the executive branch. The definition offered by the Joint Committee is an interesting one:

> . . . it is intended that the cooperating nation must have achieved considerably more than a theoretical knowledge of atomic-weapons design, or the testing of a limited number of atomic weapons. It is intended that the cooperating nation must have achieved a capability on its own of fabricating a variety of atomic weapons, and constructed and operated the necessary facilities, including weapons research and development laboratories, weapons-manufacturing facilities, a weapon-testing station, and trained personnel to operate each of these facilities.[37]

It was also "intended," as has already been pointed out, that only Great Britain be the beneficiary of this legislation. It is also clear that the architects of this less than subtle legislation were convinced that the law was so constructed as to skirt the proliferation problem. Nevertheless, the concept of a "special" nuclear relationship concealed in the legislation seemingly encourages other countries to duplicate the British effort, and can only be described as inconsistent with United States efforts to discourage all forms of nuclear proliferation. United States efforts in 1966 to include an inspection clause in a renewal of a 1954 bilateral agreement with Britain under which the United States has helped the British in the peaceful atomic energy field points up the dilemma for the United States when it attempts to bring policy in line with principle. The principle is an across-the-board imposition of international safeguards on all nations receiving United States aid to their peaceful atomic energy program; the policy is to discriminate against the nuclear "have-nots." An attempt to rectify this discrepancy in the "peaceful" atomic energy field met with British resistance.[38]

Of all the costs of this policy of nuclear discrimination none has been higher than that which the United States has paid in its post-1958 relationship with France. If President Eisenhower and John

Foster Dulles actually intended to use the 1958 modifications to the atomic energy legislation to extend increased nuclear cooperation to France, as well as Britain, such intentions were rapidly altered after the full blast of Congressional and AEC resistance was encountered, particularly during the June hearing on amending the McMahon Act.

By the time Secretary Dulles met President de Gaulle in June of 1958, Secretary Dulles' "talking points," as drafted by the Secretary himself, revealed that any plans for sharing with our "allies" had been quietly shelved. In his conversation with de Gaulle, the Secretary was to come right to the point about France's nuclear aspirations:

> The United States would have no objection to France becoming a nuclear power, if the nuclear race would stop there. . . . We did not encourage or help the UK nuclear program, believing that if each allied nation seeks independently to develop itself into a nuclear power, there would be bankruptcy everywhere and no real strength anywhere. . . .
>
> We believe that the utmost importance should be given to trying to devise a system which will assure that the free world will have adequate and dependable nuclear capacity both in terms of quantity and quality, and do this on terms that would deny nuclear power where it might be subject to possible irresponsible use.[39]

This meeting with General de Gaulle was a major turning point in the course of United States policy toward the spread of nuclear weapons. It also marks the beginning of deterioration of United States relations with France. In April of 1966 French Premier Georges Pompidou, during a debate before the French National Assembly on France's decision to break with NATO, referred to this June, 1958, meeting with obvious bitterness. When asked by M. Pleven why France had not asked the United States for some kind of help for its nuclear weapons that Britain was beginning to receive under the amendments to the McMahon Act (since, as has been pointed out, France was equally qualified), Pompidou replied:

> "Well, gentlemen, that is not politics, but wishful thinking. You will then excuse me from giving details to the Assembly. I will bring up a simple personal memory. I had the opportunity to attend a meeting at which this type of question was raised, between General de Gaulle and Mr. John Foster Dulles in—remember this date—June, 1958. I will

simply say what I learned there, not without some surprise—at the time, I undoubtedly had your naïve innocence, M. Pleven—the firm and definitive conviction that never would the American leadership ever permit the subject [of France sharing equally with Britain under the benefits of the 1958 amendments] to be broached. That conviction has never since had the chance to be shaken.[40]

France had thus received Mr. Dulles' pointed message that French nuclear weapons power "might be subject to possible irresponsible use." And from 1958 on the United States policy of maintaining a non-proliferation policy while simultaneously fostering a "special (nuclear) relationship" with Great Britain has undermined international confidence in the sincerity of our non-proliferation stand and embittered one of our staunchest Allies.

The behavior of the Eisenhower administration in its bilateral relations over the nuclear weapons issue was closely paralleled by its efforts in the international arena of the United Nations. In the days before any increase in the number of nuclear "entities" (a term of art which found its way into an American draft non-proliferation treaty) was considered a cause for international alarm, Secretary Dulles told the United Nations General Assembly that the United States made important distinctions between "kinds" of potential nuclear powers. As he said to the General Assembly on October 7, 1957 (three days after Sputnik): "We want to end the risk that nuclear weapons will be spread promiscuously throughout the world, giving irresponsible persons a power for evil that is appalling to contemplate."[41] This suggestion that the United States was not opposed to all forms of nuclear spread was well rooted in the American performance in the United Nations. Because of changes in American policy it reflects, the United States voting record in the United Nations on various non-proliferation resolutions is worth recounting.

In explaining American policy on the proliferation question United States officials have recently made much of our enthusiastic support of the so-called "Irish" resolution of 1961. The resolution on the prevention of widespread dissemination of nuclear weapons was unanimously adopted by the General Assembly of the United Na-

tions on December 4, 1961. The key paragraph in this resolution—
1665 (XVI)—calls upon all States, "and in particular upon the States
at present possessing nuclear weapons, to use their best endeavours
to secure the conclusion of an international agreement containing
provisions under which the nuclear States would undertake to refrain from relinquishing control of nuclear weapons and from transmitting the information necessary for their manufacture to States
not possessing such weapons, and provisions under which States
not possessing nuclear weapons would undertake not to manufacture
or otherwise acquire control of such weapons."[42] This resolution
was embraced by both the Soviet Union and the United States, and
has since 1961 been at least the psychological departure point for
all discussions on a non-proliferation treaty.

Long neglected in any official recounting of the nuclear dissemination question, however, is the curious, and most revealing,
history of Ireland's dogged determination in the years before 1961
to do something about the spread of nuclear weapons. For it was in
response to Irish efforts in the United Nations that the United States
proved equally determined either to nullify Ireland's pre-1961 resolutions or to mold them in such a way as to become consistent with
American policy. That is, consistent with the policy of resisting any
restraints on the use we choose to make of our nuclear knowledge
and weapons.

In October of 1958, the Chairman of the Irish delegation to the
United Nations, Mr. Frank Aiken, submitted for consideration of the
First Committee (the United Nations Committee charged with disarmament matters) a draft resolution on the dangers of the further
dissemination of nuclear weapons.[43] This draft resolution in the
operative paragraphs called for the establishment of an ad hoc committee to study the dangers inherent in a further spread of nuclear
weapons and to recommend appropriate measures to the General
Assembly at its next session. It was the second paragraph of the
preamble to the resolution that caused some very painful moments
for the American and Western European delegations. This paragraph
stated that the General Assembly recognizes "that the danger now
exists that an increase in the number of States possessing nuclear
weapons may occur, aggravating international tension. . . ."[44]

At the same time that he initiated this resolution, the Irish

Foreign Minister offered an amendment to another draft resolution already under consideration. This resolution was designed to pave the way for the establishment of a Seventeen Power Conference on the Discontinuance of Nuclear Weapons Tests. Mr. Aiken's amendment to the Seventeen Power draft resolution urged "that the parties involved in these negotiations [i.e., the Seventeen Power Conference on the Discontinuance of Nuclear Weapons Tests] shall not supply other states with nuclear weapons while these negotiations are taking place and during the suspension of tests that may result therefrom."[45]

In advancing the Irish resolution and the Irish amendment to the Seventeen Power draft resolution, Foreign Minister Aiken pursued an argument that is worth quoting *in extenso* because of its relevance to American foreign policy both past and present: "Remember that both parties would be free, according to our proposals, pending a general agreement on disarmament, to hold nuclear weapons anywhere in any allied territory that wishes to hold it. The supposed advantage which might be sacrificed would be that of handing over these weapons into ownership and control of an ally. I submit that the potential loss of this supposed advantage is scarcely worthy of being described as a risk. It is more in the nature of a hypothetical military inconvenience; but even if we agreed to regard it as a risk, it is surely insignificant in comparison with the risks on the other side and what can be won by such an agreement, for—and this is an important aspect of the question to which I would invite the Committee's special attention—the agreement by the nuclear powers not to transfer these weapons is essential if the non-nuclear powers generally will not consent to refrain from exercising their right to produce the weapons as long as nuclear Powers are not bound by a corresponding obligation to refrain from transferring.

"The two points of our proposals are, therefore, interdependent, and the prime responsibility for checking the wider dissemination of nuclear weapons rests on the present nuclear powers, and they can never get rid of their responsibility before history."[46]

Henry Cabot Lodge was the American Ambassador to the United Nations in 1958. Ambassador Lodge's response to the Irish proposal for a non-transfer pledge during the impending disarmament negotiations and an ad hoc United Nations committee to make recommendations on the proliferation question was straightforward enough: the United States would have to vote against the resolution and amendments. The reasons given for this position were artfully obscure. On a non-transfer proposal the United States could not "accept any obligation, the observance of which cannot be verified"; as for the *ad hoc* committee to study the transfer of nuclear weapons Lodge alleged that "this [Committee] would but complicate matters and duplicate the work of the Disarmament Committee."[47] In contrast, French Representative Jules Moch was more direct in his statement rejecting both proposals: Moch said that for reasons "which are readily understandable . . . we will not agree to being excluded from the nuclear powers, even while others continue to increase their stockpiles and, with these stockpiles, the dangers and risks of war."[48]

Presumably in response to this barrage of criticism, the Irish delegation withdrew its amendments to the Seventeen Power draft resolution on October 31st. As for the Irish resolution on non-dissemination, Aiken also withdrew this draft, but not before calling for a separate vote on the second paragraph of the preamble. This paragraph called for recognition by the General Assembly of the dangers of a further spread of nuclear weapons. It is significant in light of the contemporary United States policy on nuclear proliferation that the American delegation did not vote in favor of the Irish motion, but abstained. As a result, the final vote on the Irish motion was 37 in favor (including the Soviet Bloc), none against, and 44 abstentions (including the United States and all the other NATO members).[49]

Although Mr. Lodge was publicly evasive on the reasons for the United States unhappiness over the Irish proposals, the reasons for the United States displeasure were clear enough. As has been mentioned, in 1958 the view from Washington was disturbing. The Soviet's Sputnik triumph in late 1957, and subsequent emplacement of Soviet missiles aimed at Europe, had unsettled both Washington and Western Europe. In a secret State Department background paper prepared in January of 1958 for Secretary of State Dulles' use before an executive session of the Senate Foreign Relations Committee, the Department showed its concern: "European confidence has been somewhat shaken by fears of a possible U.S. reduction or withdrawal of forces, evidence of Soviet prowess in the missile and earth satellite fields, and our 'Vanguard' fiasco.

". . . NATO over the last 14 months or so has experienced difficulties of adjustment and a certain 'crisis of confidence.' The temporary breach due to Suez has been largely repaired. Yet since October 4, 1957, there has been growing concern as to NATO's ability to meet the Soviet challenge (Sputnik, ICBM)."[50] The memorandum goes on to say that these fears and uncertainties have been partially dispelled by the United States making available "nuclear delivery systems, including the IRBM."[51]

One result of this general appraisal of the West's security problems was the decision of the United States to deploy nuclear weapons (IRBM's—Thors and Jupiters) to Europe. Unlike the application of some of 1958 amendments to the atomic energy legislation, the emplacement of American nuclear weapons involved no discrimination; under the custodial system the French were as welcome as the British. Acting under the authority of this amended law, the United States entered into a series of bilateral nuclear stockpile arrangements with over half of our NATO allies. Basically these arrangements provided the authority for the release of American nuclear weapons stored in Europe to the appropriate NATO commanders in the event of hostilities.

Our problems with liberalizing our alliance nuclear relationships in the interest of general Western security were immensely complicated by Soviet Premier Khrushchev's decision in March of 1958 to suspend testing unilaterally. As has already been mentioned, the United States felt compelled to drop the idea of beating the Russians to the punch on a suspension of testing in large part because of the sensitivities and plans of the British. This 1958 position on testing reflected not only the often disabling effects of our "special relationship" with the British, but the sense of national insecurity the U.S. felt in 1958. For a brief moment Western confidence in the effectiveness of the American deterrent system was shaken.

Clearly, at this uncertain juncture, a non-proliferation resolution would have been, at best, an awkward psychological barrier to the type of nuclear arrangements we were negotiating; at worst, a direct threat to our national security.

In the interest of security, then, the United States in the 1950's put flexibility in the use of our nuclear weapons above the first fretful international efforts to erect barriers to the acquisition of nuclear weapons. As a consequence, the United States initial response to the Soviet suspension of testing was to advance an obviously unacceptable proposal requiring material inspection before the United States would agree to follow suit. Our rejection of the 1958 Irish resolution was a part of the same package, whereby the United States was determined to thwart any international efforts to restrict our full use of our nuclear weapons resources.

This "NATO first" policy can certainly be challenged on many grounds but it does have appealing virtues of clarity of purpose and of a well-ordered ledger of national priorities. It is ironic, then, that in the spring of 1958, at the very moment when our "NATO first" policy reached its high water mark when Eisenhower asked Congress for authority for a major extension of nuclear cooperation to "friendly countries," the first traces of doubt about our nuclear policy began to plague Washington.

The first real doubts came in the spring of 1958, when the White House began to realize that Congress would not consent to a major extension of nuclear cooperation to any country but Great Britain. Subsequently France made it clear that despite this rebuff it was going to defy Washington and build a national atomic force. This unpleasant prospect came at a time when the United States was also beginning to suspect that we had over-reacted to Sputnik, that, in fact, we had the capability of handling the Russian missile threat without the aid of allies. Finally, Washington came to the conclusion that our "atoms for peace" approach to halting the spread of nuclear weapons was not only ineffective but was actually helping countries to develop at least a "threshold" nuclear capability. The net effect of all these disquieting developments was to move the United States in the direction of an active non-proliferation policy.

The first significant breach in the United States' position of insisting on the uninhibited use of its nuclear weapons assets came in 1959 when the first attempt was made to make a distinction between the "control" of nuclear weapons and the "possessing" of such weapons. The issue which precipitated this change seems to have been another Irish attempt to push through the United Nations one more variety of their non-proliferation resolutions.

The resolution the Irish presented to the United Nations in 1959 on the prevention of a worldwide dissemination of nuclear weapons was adopted on November 16, 1959, by a vote of 66-0-13. In an almost complete reversal of form, the Soviet Union and the Eastern European countries, and significantly enough France, abstained while the United States and all the other NATO countries voted in favor.[52] The resolution itself introduced for the first time the idea of "control" of nuclear weapons as opposed to "ownership" or possession. It will be recalled that in the earlier Irish resolution the parties were called upon not to "supply other states with nuclear weapons." This time the Irish non-proliferation resolution called upon "the powers producing nuclear weapons to refrain from handing over *control* of such weapons to any nation not possessing them and whereby the powers not possessing such weapons would refrain from manufacturing them."[53]

Whether this particular formulation was inspired by the American delegation is not known. Whatever the origins of this important modification to the early Irish resolution, the language of the 1959 resolution was tailored to the developing American position on the proliferation question, that is, willingness to pledge adherence to any doctrine creating barriers to any additional independent nuclear forces but maintaining the right to provide information, weapons, and technology to any established nuclear force and to provide weapons and training to any non-nuclear power as long as the United States maintained "control" of the firing system.

As could be expected, the Soviet Union strenuously opposed this resolution. The Soviet representative, Mr. Kuznetsov, charged that the resolution not only failed to provide a means of halting the spread of nuclear weapons but ". . . in reality tacitly approves this development."[54] France joined the Soviet Union and the Eastern European States in opposing the resolution which was finally approved November 20, 1959.

In the fall of 1960 the Irish once more indulged their penchant for pushing resolutions on non-proliferation. On October 31, 1960, the Irish delegation submitted a draft resolution. This resolution called upon the powers, not only to "refrain from relinquishing control of such weapons to any nations not possessing them" but also to refrain from transmitting the "information necessary for their manufacture."[55] The vote on this resolution is interesting, bearing in mind that in such matters to abstain is to disapprove. The Irish resolution (1576 [XV]) was approved by the General Assembly by a vote of 68 for, none against, and 26 abstaining. For the first time a number of our NATO Allies other than France voted against the United States position. Canada, Denmark, Iceland, and Norway joined the Soviet Bloc in voting for the resolution while France joined the United States and the rest of NATO in abstaining.

In explaining the United States vote, Mr. Francis Wilcox, the American delegate, said on December 19, 1960, that the Irish resolution unfortunately "calls for an unverified commitment of indefinite duration." Moreover, Mr. Wilcox contended that "the nuclear Powers cannot expect other nations indefinitely to deny to themselves such weapons as they may believe are required for their defense if they—the nuclear Powers—refuse to accept the responsibility of halting their own build-up of nuclear weapons and refuse to begin the process of their destruction. One of our concerns with this draft resolution, therefore, is that it does not recognize the central responsibility of the nuclear Powers."[56] There is no faulting the point offered here that any formal non-proliferation agreement would be an unfair burden on the non-nuclear states, unless significant progress is made in the general disarmament area. Indeed, the argument made by Mr. Wilcox has also been made in more recent discussions of a non-proliferation treaty by India and Sweden. The paradox in 1960 was, however, that at the same time the United States was making this argument, the countries whose interests Mr. Wilcox was defending were voting for the resolution.

A better explanation for the United States opposition to this resolution can be found in the well-established opposition of the Eisenhower Administration to any restrictions on the transfer of American nuclear technology by recalling what was going on in Paris in December of 1960.

The fall of 1960 was a period of international speculation on plans and proposals the United States was considering for the control and use of nuclear weapons within the alliance. This speculation was compounded by the arrival of John F. Kennedy and a Democratic administration. General Norstad, as the Supreme Allied Commander of Europe, had already expressed his military opinion that Europe needed medium range ballistic missiles (MRBM's) in addition to the Jupiters and Thors. This stated requirement came at a time when the United States was deciding how best to meet a growing European demand for a more important voice in the nuclear management of the alliance.

It seems clear that in December of 1960 President Eisenhower's lame-duck administration was not willing to prejudice the future of any nuclear arrangement the United States might make with its NATO Allies by subscribing to the Irish resolution.

During its eight years the Eisenhower administration resisted all restrictions on the use of America's nuclear weapons resources. The opposition of Congress and the AEC, however, prevented President Eisenhower and Secretary Dulles from extending the privileges of Britain's enhanced "special relationship" to our other allies, particularly France. In reaching for this important option, the White House doubly failed. It failed to achieve its objective of sharing our knowledge with "friendly countries," and in so failing it both dramatized and inadvertently exacerbated the nuclear discrimination within the Atlantic Alliance. Blocked in its objectives here, the White House seized and doggedly protected the "control" vs. "possession" concept in order to give the United States maximum flexibility in the emplacement of its nuclear weapons.

The stage was now set for the Kennedy administration to have a try at reconciling the demands of alliance relationships with a growing national concern over the spread of nuclear weapons.

II

Kennedy and Johnson:
NATO and Geneva

> This obsession with the "Nth country," the nation that
> by manufacturing its own nuclear weapons would upset
> the present rules of the game by putting an end to the
> thermonuclear duopoly, explains the dogmatic opposition—
> almost unanimously shared by all United States analysts—
> to the spread of nuclear arms.—*Raymond Aron, 1963*

When President Kennedy arrived in the White House he soon made
it clear he intended to usher in a period of energetic opposition to the
further spread of nuclear weapons and of delicate experimentation
with nuclear relationships within the Atlantic Alliance. In the process, however, he brought to the surface many of the contradictory
elements in American policy toward the spread of nuclear weapons.
Moreover, an analysis of negotiations leading to the signing of the
Test Ban Treaty and the tabling of the non-proliferation treaty—
President Johnson's contribution—suggests that United States efforts
to control the spread of nuclear weapons have been hampered not
only by a confusion of priorities and the application of universal
solutions to selective problems, but by the way the negotiations
were handled.

In contrast to President Eisenhower's understated proliferation
policy, Kennedy raised the issue to a place of high national concern.
The Eisenhower Administration, even after the affront to France in

1958, maintained a public position of the primacy of alliance relationships coupled with a selective resistance to the spread of nuclear weapons. In practice, the Eisenhower Administration sought to maintain its monopoly over the nuclear defense of the West while holding open Washington's options to use its nuclear weapons assets as the situation dictated. What the Kennedy Administration brought to what had become by 1960 a de facto policy of supporting the nuclear "elect" was an attempt, first, to pacify our non-nuclear allies by giving them a greater voice in the management of the nuclear affairs of the alliance; and, second, to perpetuate the established nuclear powers control of nuclear arms by getting, in President Kennedy's words, "the nuclear genie back in the bottle" through a test ban and an active non-proliferation policy.

The contradictory elements in President Kennedy's policy were most painfully manifested in the short and unhappy life of the Atlantic multilateral force. Here the President simply was unable or unwilling to determine his priorities, and consequently ended up with a policy of attempting to blend the unblendable, that is, a continuation of our "special relationship" with Britain, an almost theological position that "all" nuclear spread was bad, and hints of support for the formation of an European nuclear force. In the ensuing diplomatic and political melee the Germans were talked to as though the MLF was the first step toward a European nuclear force, while the British (and the Soviets) were assured of quite the opposite; the British were given the means at Nassau to remain a nuclear "power" while the rest of Europe was told that the collective concept of the MLF was far more sensible for world security than the national solution of an independent nuclear force. Furthermore, the "good" Germans, who were told that the MLF was a means of sublimating nuclear aspirations the country had no idea it had, ended up feeling deprived of what they really wanted—an assured deterrent against the Soviet medium range ballistic missile threat to Europe. In the process, increased West German interest in nuclear weapons may have been created by the very multilateral scheme intended to quiet that interest.

Seen only in terms of the demands of many Europeans to have a greater voice in the management of the nuclear affairs of the alliance, the MLF proposal was a sound initiative. The Kennedy admin-

istration sought to avoid the "promiscuous" spread of nuclear weapons by suggesting ways of channeling European energies into a
collective nuclear force, even holding out the possibility that the
United States would support an independent European force. As
early as September of 1960 Kennedy wrote: "This inevitable trend
[the spread of nuclear knowledge and weapons]must be effectively
and responsibly organized." At the same time Kennedy went on record
as favoring a "new approach to the organization of NATO" and suggesting that the Europeans "may wish to create a NATO deterrent,
supplementary to our own, under a NATO nuclear treaty."[1]

The general direction of the Kennedy administration on the
nuclear management issue was already marked out during the last
days of President Eisenhower's term. At the December, 1960, NATO
ministerial meeting, Secretary of State Christian Herter first suggested the idea of an MRBM multilateral force. (It should be noted
at this point that the same day the NATO communiqué on the multilateral MRBM force was released—December 19, 1960—Mr. Wilcox
of the United States abstained on the Irish resolution on non-
proliferation.) A few months later, in May, 1961, President Kennedy
elaborated the idea of a NATO multilateral force in suggesting "the
possibility of eventually establishing a NATO seaborne missile force,
which would be truly multilateral in ownership and control. . . ."[2]
And with this opening the United States embarked on a policy of
creating a salve for the European irritation over the state of the
nuclear management of the Alliance, a salve which actually became,
in the words of a report of Senator Jackson's Subcommittee on Government Operations, a "five year itch." When President Kennedy in
his Ottawa speech in May, 1961, raised the possibility of Europe's
sharing in the management of the Alliance's nuclear weapons he not
only acknowledged that the Alliance's nuclear weapons relationships
should be overhauled but he opened the way to a refinement of the
distinction between the "control" and the "ownership" of nuclear
weapons. This refinement is the so-called "European option," a concept that has bedeviled the United States ever since.

The idea of a "European option," the label given to the idea
that some day Europe may want its own European nuclear force, has
its roots, if it has roots anywhere, in a speech given by McGeorge
Bundy in Copenhagen in September of 1962. Mr. Bundy promised:

"No one should suppose that we are unwilling to share in this grim responsibility whenever the responsibility is truly shared. It would also be wrong to suppose that the reluctance which we feel with respect to individual, ineffective, and unintegrated forces would be extended automatically to a European force, genuinely unified and multilateral, and effectively integrated with our own necessarily predominant strength in the whole nuclear defense of the Alliance. . . . If it should turn out that a genuinely multilateral European deterrent, integrated with ours in NATO, is what is needed and wanted, it will not be a veto from the Administration in the United States which stands in the way. . . ."[3]

The Multilateral Force was thus envisioned as a means of satisfying European desires to have a larger share in the nuclear defense of the Alliance by providing a means by which they could, at least initially, "own" but not "control" nuclear weapons. Such a proposal, in American eyes, was perfectly consistent with the 1959 and 1961 Irish resolutions, which drew a distinction between "control" and "possession." The 1960 resolution, on the other hand, which went beyond this distinction and called into question the concept of the transfer of "information," was rejected by the United States. Given the enthusiasm with which the Kennedy administration lobbied for the collective approach, it was most unfortunate that at almost the same moment this campaign was at its height, the strong strain of equivocation and contradiction that has marred the United States non-proliferation policy since 1958 again showed itself.

In November of 1962 the Defense Department informed the British Government that the United States Skybolt air-to-surface ballistic missile program would have to be canceled. Because Britain was counting on this system to extend the strategic credibility of its V-bombers, a diplomatic donnybrook ensued, leading to the Nassau meeting in late December of 1962. At this meeting the United States, in keeping with the special nuclear relationship it had developed with Britain, agreed to keep Britain as a nuclear power by making available on a continuing basis Polaris missiles—without the warheads—for British submarines.

The inconsistency of this Polaris offer with a collective solution to Europe's nuclear weapons problems has recently been pointed out by Dr. Robert R. Bowie:

I feel that to propose something like a collective force on the one hand, and then go ahead with the Nassau agreement on the other, wasn't a consistent policy. One of the purposes of the MLF was to provide a collective solution instead of national solutions for nuclear sharing. And if you went ahead and built up the national British force, that would cut across the collective concept and strengthen the position of those who don't want an MLF or any other kind of collective force.[4]

President Kennedy's insistence on continuing the special relationship with the British was not the only United States inconsistency which contributed to the demise of the MLF. The White House's efforts to please both the British and the West Germans (and not offend the Soviets) led American officials to describe the MLF to the Germans as the first step toward a European nuclear force, while confiding to the British and the Soviets the very opposite impression. The British and the Soviets quite obviously wanted to prevent any dilution of nuclear duopoly (or triopoly if the British had their way). Rather than facing up to the basic incompatibility of West German and Soviet/U.K. positions, American officials tried to cling to the idea of a "European Option" while insisting that the United States opposed all forms and varieties of proliferation. This problem lasted until 1967 when President Johnson decided that a non-proliferation pact was more important than holding open in the United States draft treaty the option of a collective force for Europe.

By the spring of 1963 it was clear that the effort to organize European nuclear talents and ambitions into a collective force that would be reconcilable with a policy of non-proliferation had failed. And with the failure Kennedy began to push very hard to erect less subtle barriers to the spread of nuclear weapons. Beginning in 1963, the United States' regional political-military relationships became increasingly interwoven with our strenuous efforts to raise technological barriers to the acquisition of nuclear weapons. Unfortunately, this effort was marred not only by Washington's difficulty in accepting the fact that an active non-proliferation policy could be irreconcilable with regional security arrangements, but by the way the Test Ban Treaty and, to a lesser extent, the way the Non-Proliferation Treaty is being handled. Long accustomed to dealing with the Soviet Union at the summit level, the United States has allowed itself to carry over into an entirely new international climate the negotiating habits of the era when the United States and the Soviet Union and Great Britain had an unchallenged corner on nuclear arms. As a result, our allies and those of the Soviet Union, as well as the unaligned countries, were inadequately consulted during the critical negotiations leading to the Test Ban Treaty. These countries, who were asked to agree to a critical act of national self-denial (at least at the time the Test Ban Treaty was ratified), found themselves confronted in 1963 with a *fait accompli*, the consequences of which are felt to this day. In the case of the Non-Proliferation Treaty, the non-nuclear powers have been "consulted" and informed almost on a daily basis. The problem has been that the non-nuclear powers at Geneva or New York have not participated in the drafting of a treaty. This has set up a "we" and "they" relationship in contrast to the highly successful negotiations for the Outer Space Treaty where all the members of the comparable UN committee actively drafted, and subsequently defended, the draft treaty.

On January 18, 1968 the United States and the Soviet Union presented the Disarmament Conference with an identical and complete text of a draft treaty to halt the spread of nuclear weapons. The Geneva Conference, after considering the draft, will report to the UN General Assembly.

Now that the negotiations have moved beyond the complete control of the major powers, the United States and the Soviet Union will begin to see the consequences of restricting the participation of the other potential parties to the treaty in the drafting process.

Given the problems of negotiating international agreements affecting nuclear weapons, it is no wonder that President Kennedy decided to go outside the United Nations framework to negotiate a Test Ban Treaty.

When President Kennedy in March of 1963 spoke of the possibility that in the 1970's the President of the United States would be forced to face a world "in which 15 or 20 or 25 nations may have these weapons" he was reflecting the prevailing attitude of the early 1960's which emphasized nuclear "capability" rather than "intention." Deeply troubled by this prospect, it is no wonder that the President took a position of unrelenting hostility to the spread of nuclear weapons. In a series of steps—the appointment of John J.

McCloy as his adviser on disarmament and Arthur Dean as the new principal negotiator at Geneva, the creation of the Arms Control and Disarmament Agency, and the tabling of a disarmament proposal in September of 1961 that for the *first time* included a specific non-proliferation clause—President Kennedy soon made it clear that he intended to check the spread of nuclear weapons.

Although President Kennedy did offer a non-proliferation proposal in his September 25, 1961, "Program for Complete and General Disarmament," which called for states owning nuclear weapons not to relinquish control of such weapons or transmit information to non-nuclear states, and also backed the 1961 Irish resolution on non-proliferation, the President concentrated on achieving a nuclear test ban. Two aspects of the test ban effort are particularly significant for the non-proliferation question: the way this treaty was handled and the consequences for our relations with the non-nuclear powers; and the effectiveness of the Test Ban Treaty as a technological barrier to the further spread of nuclear weapons.

Despite President Kennedy's efforts to bring a new impetus to efforts to achieve a test ban treaty he found himself in the spring of 1963 seemingly no closer to an agreement than two years before. In August of 1962, in order to get around the underground testing stalemate, the United States tabled a separate treaty which would have stopped all tests in outer space, in the atmosphere, and under water. This draft treaty and an alternate comprehensive treaty were debated at length at the Eighteen Nation Disarmament Conference in Geneva and at the Seventeenth General Assembly of the United Nations. Each of these treaties was rejected by the Soviet Union in 1962. Frustrated by this deadlock, President Kennedy, in a speech at American University on June 10, 1963, announced that he had come to an agreement with Chairman Khrushchev and Prime Minister Macmillan to begin shortly in Moscow high level discussions "looking toward early agreement on a comprehensive test ban." On July 2, in a speech delivered in Berlin, Chairman Khrushchev expressed the willingness of the Soviet Union "to conclude an agreement banning nuclear tests in the atmosphere, in outer space and under water" combined with a nonaggression pact between the NATO countries and the Warsaw Pact. This exchange was virtually all the other countries of the world knew of impending Moscow negotiations;

and the manner in which the negotiations themselves were handled in Moscow was guaranteed to stimulate the fears of those who felt that the three major powers had defied the established forum of test ban negotiations and were proceeding, without consultation, to present the rest of the world with a *fait accompli.*

President Kennedy was aware of the possible consequences for the United States alliance relationship of the way the negotiations were being handled. He told his staff at the time: "I have some cash in the bank in West Germany and am prepared to draw down on it if you think I should."[5] What Kennedy was referring to was the enormous amount of good will he had won in West Germany during his trip there in June of 1963. Before the Nuclear Test Ban was finally ratified by West Germany, Kennedy would indeed have to draw down heavily on that good will. What concerned many friends of the United States was the unusual secrecy drawn over the Moscow negotiations. The American team was headed not by the Director of the Arms Control and Disarmament Agency, but by Averell Harriman with support from Carl Kaysen of the White House, Adrian Fisher from the Arms Control and Disarmament Agency, John McNaughton from the Defense Department, and William Tyler from the State Department.

Moreover, concerned non-participants could hardly have had much confidence that Great Britain would be an effective champion of the interests of the nations not represented. By July of 1963, Prime Minister Macmillan was so personally committed to a test ban treaty, and so in need of an international success to divert British public attention from the Profumo case, that Britain's role of "honest broker" was not a realistic one. Arthur Schlesinger's description of the chief British negotiator at Moscow, Lord Hailsham, is appropriate here: "The choice fell on Quintin Hogg, then Lord Hailsham, Minister of Science and an accomplished if impetuous lawyer. (Macmillan later confided to newspapermen that he had sent Hailsham because he thought he might amuse Khrushchev.) Hailsham, relying on the British amateur tradition, was ill prepared on the technicalities of the problem and was consumed by a desire to get a treaty at almost any cost."[6]

During the negotiations, friendly foreign diplomats, who are usually well briefed by the State Department on the general course of major power negotiations affecting their interests, were kept completely in the dark—as were all but a few top officials in the United States Government. All cables to and from Moscow were cleared through Kennedy himself and incoming cables were passed to Secretary Rusk, Undersecretary Ball, John McCone of the Central Intelligence Agency, and Secretary McNamara on an "eyes-only" basis—that is, for their eyes alone. It is no wonder that the Adenauer government, in Ted Sorensen's words, took "an alarmist attitude" toward the whole procedure.[7]

The singlemindedness of the Kennedy administration to push the negotiations through to a successful conclusion was a spectacular success. Six weeks after the American University speech the Nuclear Test Ban Treaty was initiated; on September 24 the Senate gave its consent to ratification by a vote of 80–19; and by the end of the year over one hundred nations had signed the treaty (important exceptions, of course, were France and Communist China). A success without question—but not without its costs in the confidence of the nonnuclear powers, and not without its troublesome legacies to the field of the peaceful uses of nuclear power and to the question of the recognition of East Germany.

A comparison of the text of the United States treaty tabled at the Eighteen Nation Disarmament Conference on August 27, 1962, which was the working text at Moscow, and the final text initiated at Moscow on August 5, 1963, shows that the United States consented to two important concessions pressed for by the Soviet Union: a concession on the status of East Germany, and the concession to drop the United States position on peaceful nuclear explosives.

In the first case, a compromise was struck by which the Soviet Union's desire to upgrade the status of East Germany was met by a device which designated the United States, the United Kingdom, and the Soviet Union as depositary governments in order that states not recognized by one or more of the parties (such as East Germany) could formally accede to the treaty. In the past, in those few cases where the United States and East Germany were party to the same convention, the United States had responded to notice of East Germany's accession from the single depositary government, such as Switzerland in the case of the 1949 Geneva Convention, by stating that the United States does not recognize the "German Democratic Republic" but notes its intention to apply the convention.

As a result of the device agreed to at Moscow, the United States, while firmly stating to the Congress and its Allies that this action in no way constituted tacit recognition of the East German regime, could be put in a most awkward position if an amending conference is called. For under Article II of the treaty such a conference may be called if one-third of the signatories so desire.[8]

The important point here is not whether the accession clauses of the treaty elevated the status of the East German regime. However, if for no other reason than the fact that the device of using three depositary governments has been used with the Outer Space Treaty and now with the non-proliferation treaty, it is safe to say that the decision made in Moscow did open the way for a developing pattern of tacit recognition by the West of East Germany. This point can be argued, of course. What cannot be argued is that the United States acting unilaterally made a decision affecting Germany's vital interests without even consulting the West Germans. It is no wonder that the West Germans have been almost morbidly suspicious of United States intentions during the non-proliferation negotiations—to the detriment of useful dialogue between friends and allies.

If the United States unilateral decision on the means of accession to the Nuclear Test Ban Treaty caused difficulty with one friend and ally, our decision to abandon the western position on the peaceful uses of nuclear explosives has damaged our position with a multitude of aspiring non-nuclear powers and enormously complicated the non-proliferation negotiations now under way. The problem began when, at Soviet insistence, the United States dropped Article II of the August 27 draft. This article would have allowed the explosion of nuclear devices for peaceful purposes. At Moscow the Soviets were terribly suspicious that the United States would conduct advanced nuclear weapons tests under the cover of exploding nuclear devices for peaceful purposes. As a result of this pressure, the United States agreed to drop this article and amend the basic prohibitions to make certain that it was clear that "other nuclear explosions" in the specified environments were also prohibited. It is curious to note, considering the potential problem with East Germany's status if an amending conference were convened, that the United States and Moscow insisted on reducing the number of signatories necessary to amend the treaty from two-thirds of the parties to a simple majority. This was done in order to facilitate a future amendment restoring the right to detonate nuclear devices for peaceful purposes.[9]

Again, what was critical here was not whether the United States should have insisted on retaining the option of exploding nuclear devices for peaceful purposes in the atmosphere, in outer space, or under water. Kennedy simply felt that the prohibition on peaceful nuclear explosives was a necessary price to pay for a treaty. In this he may have underestimated the interest of the Soviet Union in attaining a treaty, particularly since the Soviets were almost certainly aware of how close the Chinese were in 1963 to a nuclear weapons test. Consequently, agreement on a test ban treaty in 1963 may have been the Russians' last chance to isolate the Chinese in world opinion by an international treaty prohibiting just what the Chinese were about to do. Nevertheless, the major fault with the peaceful uses of atomic energy concession was the Kennedy administration's assumption of the right to speak for all those vitally concerned with the future of the commercial uses of nuclear energy. This assumption was again a hangover from the international outlook of nuclear matters that the United States developed in the first years after the war—that is, such important decisions are better left to major powers, namely the United States and the Soviet Union. President Johnson is now coping with the difficult legacy of that attitude as he tries to persuade other nations that we must work together in controlling the uses of this new power.

Finally, there is the question of the effectiveness of the Test Ban Treaty as a technological barrier to the acquisition of nuclear weapons. From the testimony given at the time the Senate had the treaty under consideration, there appears to be no doubt that the partial test ban raised a formidable barrier to the spread of nuclear weapons. This barrier is more psychological and political than technological, however. The high confidence shown by United States officials that developing a nuclear weapon underground would be a difficult task was in part the result of that ill-founded but persistent belief on the part of many Americans that "others" are simply not as good as we are. This technological smugness has been one of the most unfortunate characteristics of the United States policy since the Second World War. That President Kennedy chose to over-sell the Test Ban Treaty as a barrier to further proliferation was probably due to a combination of this sense of the technological limitations of others and the President's anxiousness to win Congressional approval.

In President Kennedy's message to Congress, transmitting the draft of the limited test ban treaty, he emphasized the effect he hoped the treaty would have on the spread of nuclear weapons:

> While it [the test ban] cannot wholly prevent the spread of nuclear weapons to nations not now possessing them, it prohibits assistance to testing in these environments [the atmosphere, in outer space, and under water] by others; it will be signed by many other potential testers; and it is thus an important opening wedge in our effort to "get the genie back in the bottle." [10]

The argument of the Kennedy Administration that the test ban treaty would inhibit the spread of nuclear weapons was forcefully put forward by Secretary of State Dean Rusk in his testimony before the Senate Foreign Relations Committee:

> . . . The treaty will help contain the spread of nuclear weapons. We cannot guarantee it. Most of the countries with the capacity and the incentive to develop nuclear weapons over the next decade or so have already announced that they will accept the self-denying ordinance of the treaty. These countries do not include, by the way, mainland China or France.
>
> While this [treaty] does not guarantee that they will never become nuclear powers, their renunciation of atmospheric testing will act as a deterrent by making it much more difficult and expensive for them to develop nuclear weapons. [11]

Secretary of Defense McNamara was even more expansive and reassuring as he developed the argument later in the hearing:

> With testing limited to the underground environment, the potential cost of a nuclear weapons program would increase sharply for all signatory states. And since testing underground is not only more costly but also more difficult and time-consuming, the proposed treaty would retard progress in weapons development in cases where the added cost and other factors were not sufficient to preclude it altogether. One of the great advantages of this treaty is that it will have the effect of retarding the spread of nuclear weapons. [12]

It is important to subject the logic behind the argument that the partial test ban will "have the effect of retarding the spread of nuclear weapons" to careful scrutiny. The proposition has been advanced in this study that certain technological and political assumptions of the late 1940's with regard to nuclear weapons were not only faulty at the time but have persisted to a point where they inhibit a realistic appraisal of the pace, scope, and implications of "nuclear proliferation." If the testimony by members of the Kennedy administration on the expected retardative effect of the limited test ban on the spread of nuclear weapons is any indication, we were almost certainly exaggerating the technological barriers to a weapons program then as we had so often in the past.

The logic behind the argument that because underground testing is allegedly "more costly," "time consuming," and technically more difficult than atmospheric testing, the test ban will retard proliferation is questionable even if we assume that these "costs" are as described. First of all, it may not be necessary to "test" in the accepted sense of the word. It should not be forgotten that the first U-235 bomb was "tested" over Hiroshima, and the first plutonium bomb, although tested as a device at Alamagordo, was tested as a weapon over Nagasaki.

Nevertheless, assuming that testing is necessary, one should consider the physical circumstances of most of the 100-plus nations who signed the treaty prohibiting nuclear detonations in the atmosphere, outer space, and under water. Just how many of the non-nuclear signatories actually have access to an adequate test range for atmospheric testing? Such countries as West Germany, Switzerland, Israel, and India, which have often been mentioned as potential nuclear powers, clearly do not have the necessary domestic sites, and if they felt the necessity to test in the atmosphere would have to rely on the use of someone else's property. On the other hand, Sweden could probably test in arctic Sweden. It is also worth recalling that both France and Communist China, who rejected the treaty, have adequate facilities for atmospheric testing—France in the South Pacific and China in the sparsely populated area of Western China. In other words, it could be argued that, quite apart from the treaty, underground testing is the only practical way open to developing a weapon.

Israel, for example, was giving up very little when it signed the test ban treaty.

But what of the argument that underground testing is more costly, diagnostically less satisfactory than testing above ground, and hampers progress in weapons development? All of this is generally true but probably not to the degree that the United States government has hopefully predicted. To begin with, the matter of the cost of underground testing is, by Secretary McNamara's own admission, not as clear-cut as his statement that "the potential cost of a nuclear weapons program would increase sharply for all signatory states" would indicate. The following exchange with Senator Sparkman, which occurred at the same Congressional hearing, throws a slightly different light on the issue of costs:

> *Senator Sparkman:* Now, you speak of the cost. If I understand your statement correctly, the cost of testing underground is higher proportionately than testing in other areas.
>
> *Secretary McNamara:* We were speaking particularly of the cost of developing tactical weapons, low-yield, low-weight warheads, and in that context it would be more costly to carry out experiments for that purpose than in the atmosphere.[13]

But what of a strategic weapon, relatively crude by Mr. McNamara's standards, with a yield in the 50 to 100 kiloton range? How much more costly would it be to test such a weapon underground than above ground? The question was, unfortunately, left unanswered during the test ban hearings.

As to the matter of the technical difficulties of testing underground, the potential nuclear aspirant has only to turn to such open publications as the transcript of a hearing of the Joint Congressional Committee on Atomic Energy on the AEC's budget for an astounding amount of technical information on how to test underground. From the hearing on the 1965 budget, for example, an interested third party could learn the following about the United States program and its progress and problems:

(1) On the basis of wide and costly experience, the United States has abandoned the technique of boring a lateral tunnel for test sites in favor of a single vertical hole.

(2) The United States uses a figure based on the cube root of

the expected maximum yield in kilotons to determine the amount of overburden or ceiling required in each of the holes to prevent venting or escape of radioactive materials.

(3) The United States is using rotary drilling bits 6 feet in diameter for its largest holes, although some of the low-yield experiments go down to 29-inch holes. Costs of the drilling ranges from a few hundred thousand dollars for a low-yield hole to as high as $3 million for larger yield deep holes.

(3) Alluvium soil is the most desirable testing medium, while if the testing is done in granite the detection range would be greater.[14]

The above is just another example of the curious manner in which the United States has handled its nuclear secrets ever since the days of the Smyth report. Strict, almost oppressive secrecy while a project is under way, then almost compulsive gabbiness, particularly when seeking Congressional approval or, better stated, appropriations. Whatever the psychology of the process, it is safe to assume that eventually there will be little left to the world's imagination as to the "secrets" of America's underground testing programs. Time, with or without the stimulus of foreign espionage, will almost certainly dispel the mysteries of underground testing.

In sum, a prohibition on atmospheric tests probably does impose a barrier for those considering a weapon. But how high this barrier is and how long it will remain so is an open question. As a witness for this view, we have only to use an excerpt from the testimony of Dr. N. E. Bradbury, Director of the Los Alamos Scientific Laboratory, before the Committee on Foreign Relations:

> Underground testing will permit, I am convinced, essentially every technical warhead development which would be possible with atmospheric testing up to yields as great as a megaton. The Hiroshima and Nagasaki bombs were [after all] in the range of 15–20 kilotons. . . . With underground testing, I believe we can develop and test whatever type of warhead may be required for an anti-ballistic missile system if one is required. Small weapons, cleaner weapons, tactical weapons, to the extent that any of these are needed and practical, can be worked on and improved.[15]

Dr. Bradbury was talking, of course, only about the United States and how the test ban would affect our nuclear weapons program. But it would be the height of ethnocentric smugness to assume that others cannot duplicate our efforts in the underground testing field. If the limited test ban is the main obstacle to further proliferation, then it is a grossly inadequate and potentially deceptive one.

If the Kennedy administration had difficulties reconciling an active non-proliferation policy with regional security arrangements and commercial nuclear interests, the problem of blending the unblendable has been even more difficult since President Johnson has made the attainment of a non-proliferation treaty a national *jihad.* In his January 27, 1966, message to the Eighteen Nation Disarmament Committee, President Johnson said the United States has ". . . with all mankind, a common interest in acting now to reduce nuclear stocks." He urged that the world must move forward "while there is yet time" with a treaty to prevent the spread of nuclear weapons—a problem he had a year before called the "gravest of all unresolved human issues."

The President's concern over the proliferation question is obviously as sincere as is his strong desire to achieve an international agreement limiting the spread of nuclear weapons. Consequently, many nations were puzzled and disturbed that President Johnson's noble intentions were blurred for so long by a United States draft treaty so obviously unacceptable to the Soviet Union. The United States' original insistence on a non-proliferation treaty that allowed for the future development with United States support of a joint European nuclear force not only made Soviet agreement unlikely, but also defied the expressed unwillingness of the U.S. Congress to authorize such an arrangement, and ignored strong indications of European lack of interest in such as U.S. sponsored force.

The language at issue in the U.S. draft non-proliferation treaty as presented on August 17, 1965, and modified on March 22, 1966, pledged each of the nuclear-weapons states "not to transfer nuclear weapons into the national control of any non-nuclear weapon state or into the control of any association of non-nuclear states," and "not to take any action which would cause an increase in the total number of states having control of nuclear weapons." The intent here was clear: to permit the European states at some point to form a nuclear-sharing arrangement into which Great Britain would merge its own nuclear forces. The United States would maintain "control" of the nuclear weapons while Britain's merging of her forces would cause no net increase in the number of nuclear powers.

This is not to say that the original Soviet draft treaty was any more realistic or negotiable. The Soviets insisted that the parties to the treaty agree that they ". . . shall not acquire control over nuclear weapons or even over their emplacement and use for units of their armed forces or personnel thereof, even of such units or personnel that are under the command of a military alliance." Such a demand was obviously aimed not at preventing the spread of nuclear weapons but at destroying present NATO nuclear arrangements.

In the process of negotiation the United States painted itself into a most uncomfortable corner through our efforts to hold open our nuclear options while simultaneously proclaiming to the world that we had no such intention. During an international television forum in 1966, Franz Joseph Strauss, West Germany's former Minister of Defense, persisted in putting one particular question to Senator Robert Kennedy, who was defending the United States draft treaty. That question was: "NATO or Geneva? What is your priority?" The question was apt, and important—but Senator Kennedy could not answer. For, at the time, the United States was moving hesitantly in a shadow area between competing policies. The results were a convoluted draft treaty that, according to one observer, could only have been written by a ball point pen mounted on a cork screw, and an international posture on nuclear proliferation that was as disturbing to our Allies as it was provocative to the Soviet Union.

The great debate within the United States has now been resolved—we have chosen Geneva over NATO nuclear sharing, at least for the short term. The basic compromise in the recent nonproliferation pact was one of the United States dropping the so-called "European option" clause in exchange for the Soviet Union withdrawing its insistence on outlawing present NATO nuclear arrangements. President Johnson has thus resolved one of the most troublesome internal contradictions in United States policy toward the spread of nuclear weapons. But he has paid at least a small price in future alliance relationship by closing out our option to assist our other allies in the nuclear weapons field, as we have assisted the British, and to participate in any future Atlantic nuclear force.

President Johnson may have other bills to pay before a nonproliferation treaty is a reality. On January 18, 1968, the Soviet Union and the United States submitted identical drafts on a non-proliferation treaty to the Eighteen Nation Disarmament Conference. This action came after months of Soviet-American negotiations which took place as the rest of the conference was left in the position of simply waiting for the United States and the Soviet Union to agree.

In the process of bringing this treaty to the negotiating table the United States made a considerable effort to consult with the countries most directly affected—particularly India, Israel, Japan, and West Germany. It is unfortunate, however, given the United States' record on the Nuclear Test Ban, that this draft treaty was not negotiated openly at the disarmament conference along the lines of the negotiations leading to the Outer Space Treaty. Instead the United States and the Soviet Union chose to negotiate bilaterally, hoping that an active program of consultation with the non-nuclear powers would be enough. Thus, the way this treaty was negotiated, while effective, will probably cause its critics in the Eighteen Nation Disarmament Conference and the United Nations to argue their positions even more strenuously in order to make it clear that they are not prepared to accept a *fait accompli* sent down from on high by the United States and the Soviet Union.

As these negotiations move through the Eighteen Nation Disarmament Conference and the General Assembly, the United States will be confronted with the individual problems of non-nuclear states—problems which at times will seem to defy collective solutions: nuclear guarantees, the issue of inspection, demands for pledges by the nuclear powers to begin to disarm, demands for a provision to permit some form of program of peaceful nuclear explosions. If the Soviet Union and the United States are prepared to give nuclear guarantees outside the framework of the treaty and to permit national nuclear explosive programs under very specific conditions of international inspection, there will probably be a treaty which India, West Germany, Israel, and Japan will sign. If the major powers do not make these concessions, at least one of the "targets" of this treaty—probably India—may refuse to sign. If this happens, both the President and particularly the United States Congress will begin to wonder whether the cure was really properly prescribed for the disease. The United States may even decide to re-evaluate its national attitudes toward the spread of nuclear weapons.

If the United States were forced to make such a re-evaluation of national attitudes, the exercise would be a healthy one. We have come to regard the spread of nuclear weapons in a special—even disturbing—way. Raymond Aron has written of the United States' current "obsession" with the problem and its "dogmatic opposition . . . to the spread of nuclear arms." Aron's choice of the language of theology to describe the United States' attitude toward the spread of nuclear weapons may be all too appropriate. There is no doubt that American policy on the spread of nuclear weapons does show strong overtones of dogmatism—dogmatism and a tendency to over-generalize about the dangers of a further spread of nuclear arms. It is almost taken for granted that any extension of the possession of nuclear weapons is, by definition, bad. As a principle, this approach is un-equivocal and total whether the offender is France, Communist China, or Sweden—nuclear immorality remains totally immoral.

Will this attitude change now that a non-proliferation pact is close to becoming a reality? The answer depends on how the United States chooses to evaluate its past experience, and how it approaches the problem of "why" nations want or do not want nuclear weapons. We have chosen an international or universal treaty as the core of our anti-proliferation strategy. Whether this strategy is well tailored to the problem can best be tested by examining the national circumstances of a few potential nuclear powers.

III

National Circumstances and Nuclear Status

> The rate at which we can expect the spread of nuclear capability to additional nations will depend upon each nation's present technology, its present industrial capacity, its level of education, and the rate at which these factors are changing. . . . By 1970 most nations with appreciable military strength will have in their arsenals nuclear weapons—strategic, tactical, or both.—*1970 Without Arms Control*, NATIONAL PLANNING ASSOCIATION, 1958.

> I am shocked that there should be even talk of violence in his presence.—The late Indian Prime Minister Lal Bahadur Shastri, pointing to a huge picture of Gandhi after listening to numerous speakers at the 1964 All-India Congress call for an Indian atomic bomb.

Secretary of Defense McNamara's forecast that in ten to twenty years "tens of nations" would be able to produce usable nuclear weapons is a way of viewing the proliferation problem that is as disturbing as it is unhelpful. If pressed on the likelihood of such a development, Mr. McNamara would probably reply that his statement referred only to "capacity," not "intention." Nevertheless, if the United States hopes to devise new methods of arranging our international dealings in a world where the threat to use nuclear explosives may come from as many as "tens of nations," then there is clearly a need to impose a more systematic way of approaching this problem than emphasizing capacity to make nuclear devices.

As more and more countries become industrialized, it is natural that Secretary McNamara would stress the ease with which more and more countries will be able to develop nuclear devices. McNamara's approach is in the best tradition of these impressive pioneer studies of the Nth Country problem done by the National Planning Association in 1958 and 1960.[1] Here the analysis centered on defining the level of industrial and economic activity required to develop nuclear weapons independently. The criteria included such indices as gross national product (greater than $100 million was considered adequate), steel production (greater than 100,000 tons), electrical power (greater than ten billion kilowatt hours per year), the existence of an adequate chemical industry (a sulfuric-acid production of more than 50,000 tons was enough), the presence of a machine industry (an automobile industry), and evidence of a capacity for major construction (a ship-building industry would do).[2] Using these indices, an industrial check list was devised comparing the capacities of 37 countries. The results were not too surprising: By way of example, Sweden, Italy, and Switzerland received a plus in all six columns, while Israel received two, Indonesia one, and Egypt two.[3]

Despite the great care taken by the distinguished members of the National Planning Association Special Project Committee to qualify and explain the limitations of such grouping, the NPA approach of grouping potential nuclear countries by economic and technical capabilities has become a permanent part of the proliferation literature. Indeed, even the expression "Nth Country problem," with "N" representing an indeterminate but clearly large number of countries which will one day make their "rendezvous with Mephistopheles," has highlighted the idea of an inexorable march from "capability" to "intention."

In recent years, studies of the proliferation problem have tended to play down the role of nuclear technology and economic capacity in any national decision to develop nuclear weapons in favor of emphasizing the delivery problem and the political factors bearing on any decision to press for nuclear weapons. Nevertheless, even the excellent study done by Leonard Beaton and John Maddox, *The Spread of Nuclear Weapons*, gives a very close look at the technical problems of developing nuclear weapons and then examines as case studies of potential nuclear countries ". . . the situation *in those countries which are most able to build a nuclear weapons system but have not done so . . .*";[4] that is, such countries as Canada, India, Communist China, Sweden, and Switzerland.[5] In another book on the spread of nuclear weapons proliferation the bulk of the study is given over to an examination of the British, French, and NATO experience with nuclear weapons. While admitting that the experience we have accumulated about existing nuclear powers may be "rendered obsolete by events," the editor of the study, R. N. Rosecrance, writes that ". . . the British case has been examined in some detail for the clues it might provide to Nth country development in other cases."[6] But what sort of clues does the British case provide? It may well be that generalizing from the British or French experience will give us a very misleading picture of future Nth country developments.

First of all, there is no question of the usefulness of an analysis of the skills of the countries potentially able to acquire nuclear weapons, as Beaton and Maddox have done, or emphasizing the experience of existing nuclear powers as a means of discerning the possible pattern of nuclear spread, as Rosecrance has done. But the question still remains, to what extent do the national circumstances of Britain or Sweden, their incentives and inhibitions in the nuclear arms field, have any particular application to India's nuclear problem, or Israel's, or Indonesia's? Will a study of Sweden's economic and technological skills and the application of the British and French nuclear experience be helpful in determining the future of India's debate on whether to acquire nuclear weapons? Will success in discouraging one country from acquiring nuclear weapons, or improving the weapons systems it already has, have much effect on the decisions of other countries?

These questions are important ones, and not only because they bear directly on the problem of estimating the nuclear future of particular countries. There is also the question of the relevance of the domino effect on nuclear proliferation. It seems clear from the grim determination with which the United States has attempted to retard the French nuclear program and dissuade the Indians from following China that we are convinced that there is more at stake here than the future of these two countries. The United States apparently feels so strongly about the nuclear future of these two countries because we believe that decisions made by France and India will be key elements in the future of the whole proliferation issue. In other words, if France should continue its success in the weapons field, if India should follow China, they will represent the first collapse in what is certain to be a nuclear domino effect throughout the world. The stakes, then, are as much symbolic as they are practical. Stop India and cause the French to renounce their nuclear aspirations and you will stop others.

There is obviously a certain amount of truth in such reasoning but the process deserves careful scrutiny lest we come to believe that a nuclear France inevitably will mean a nuclear Sweden or West Germany. What seems to be required, if we are to escape from the tendency to view the prospects for nuclear proliferation primarily in terms of the experiences of the present nuclear powers or the fearful unfolding of some Malthusian law, is to take a careful look at the special economic, political, and technological circumstances of individual countries to see if both the forces at work and the national responses form a recognizable international pattern. Five countries often mentioned in any appraisal of the "Nth" country problem are India, Japan, West Germany, Israel, and the United Arab Republic. A brief description of how these countries view their changing circumstances with regard to nuclear weapons may be useful in determining means by which the United States may be able to remove or alter the incentives to develop nuclear weapons. The Indian dilemma is a prime example of the complexities of the problem involved in any national decision to develop nuclear weapons—and, therefore, a useful place to start.

India

In March of 1967 India's former Foreign Minister, M. C. Chagla, assured the Indian Parliament that as far as India's interests were concerned: ". . . a satisfactory agreement on the non-proliferation of nuclear weapons will have to take into account the peculiar circumstances in which certain countries are placed." Bending the language of an international treaty to suit the "peculiar circumstances" is a difficult chore at best; but, in the case of India, the country's position with regard to nuclear weapons is so "peculiar" that the task calls into serious question the usefulness of universal remedies when dealing with the proliferation question.

The Lop Nor explosion in September, 1964, which marked the emergence of Communist China as a power capable of producing nuclear weapons, has opened a period of grave challenge for India. Indian initial response to the Chinese success was sounded in October, 1964, by former Prime Minister Shastri at the Cairo Conference of nonaligned nations:

> We in India stand committed to use atomic energy only for peaceful purposes and even though, in a purely technical and scientific sense, we have the capability of developing nuclear weapons, our scientists and technicians are under firm orders not to make a single experiment, not to perfect a single device which is not needed for peaceful uses of atomic energy.[7]

This statement came at a time of great national anxiety in India over the country's security. Indians were beginning to take seriously the threat of Chinese missile bases in Tibet commanding India's northern industrial belt and major transportation arteries. As one consequence, India's defense budget remains around a billion dollars yearly in an effort to equip with conventional arms an army which may reach some 825,000 men.[8] All this at a time when some 14 or 15 divisions of Chinese troops occupy approximately 14,500 square miles of territory taken from India as the spoils of the 1962 conflict.

Public debate within India over the proper response to the Chinese bomb has been particularly troubled and anguished because of the knowledge that the country has the means of following the Chinese example. To follow China into the nuclear weapons field would present no insurmountable problems for the Indians whose atomic skills Dr. Glenn Seaborg, Chairman of the United States Atomic Energy Commission, has said are as advanced as those of China. The Indian Atomic Energy Commission has, since its organization in 1954, made great strides in the development of atomic power plants. India's Atomic Energy Establishment located at Trombay has recently been named for Dr. Homi J. Bhabha, India's foremost atomic scientist until his death in 1966. The Bhabha center is one of the finest atomic energy centers in the world.

It has been estimated that India will have by 1986 more than

2 million kilowatts of installed atomic energy power, more than the planned atomic power of all other countries save the United States, France, and Great Britain.[9] Spending at a rate of around $50 million a year for atomic energy, India has at its disposal a 40 MWe Indo-Canadian reactor (CIR) which as of 1965 is fueled entirely with Indian fuel rods, also abundant ores and an ore-processing plant. Canada is assisting India with the construction of a 220,000 kilowatt reactor near the Chambal River. With the financial help of the United States, the Indians have also begun work on a 380 MWe power station at Tarapur, Bombay.[10] With the dedication in January, 1965, of a plutonium chemical separation plant, India joined that select group (with the exception of India only the present nuclear powers and the European Nuclear Energy Agency [ENEA] have such a plant) of countries which have all the necessary facilities and materials for the independent manufacture of a nuclear device.[11]

With this record of accomplishment, it is no wonder that the Chinese nuclear success stirred such controversy in India and reinforced the view of many that India is a prime candidate for nuclear status.[12]

Thus far, however, the Indian Government has resisted the pressure to develop its own atomic bomb while simultaneously pushing ahead with all programs (such as a chemical separation plant) necessary to bring India to the threshold of a weapons program.

In technical terms, the geographic circumstances of India are highly conducive to the development and underground testing of nuclear weapons. India, because of its size and the decentralization of its industrial centers and population, has less to fear from an enemy with a small stockpile of atomic weapons than, say, Israel. India would therefore be less concerned about the introduction of a limited number of atomic weapons into the area than a smaller country. Moreover, India's size, population, and industrial potential place the country in the category of those few nations who can aspire to an economic and military parity with the major powers where nuclear weapons are a symbol of that status. As Jawaharlal Nehru once put it:

Leaving these three big countries, the United States of America, the Soviet Union, and China, aside for the moment, look at the world.

There are many advanced, highly cultured countries. But if you peep into the future and if nothing goes wrong—wars and the like—the fourth country in the world is India.[13]

An added geographic incentive for the development or acquisition of nuclear weapons is India's extensive border. The need here, of course, would be for tactical nuclear weapons. From northern Kashmir to the northeastern frontier of Assam, India has 2,000 miles of border with China's Tibet as well as being faced with problems of defending itself from attacks through the western mountain states of Bhutan, Sikkim, and Nepal. A stockpile of less than one hundred tactical nuclear weapons delivered by India's *Canberra* aircraft could close these passes and destroy some of China's airfields in Tibet in a moment of national crisis when Indian troops would be hard pressed even to get into position.

Thus India's physical size, its potential for parity with the superpowers, its pattern of population and industrial dispersal, and its territorial defense problems are such that the country's physical circumstances must be counted as decidedly favoring the development or acquisition of at least tactical nuclear weapons.

India also has a great economic need for atomic energy which has lessened any possible domestic opposition to such a large program. By 1986 India will have a population of at least 700 million and will require three times as much electrical power as the country has even potentially in hydro-thermal resources.[14] Lacking in coal, under-endowed in exploitable hydro-electric power, and anxious to develop the food preservation potential in atomic radiation, India, with its increasing capacity to produce a nuclear device at minimal cost, has great incentive to pursue a broadly based atomic energy program.

On the other hand, India has staggering economic problems which clearly impose a major stumbling block if it wishes to move from atomic power plants to anything more than a crude atomic device, possibly deliverable by aircraft. Moreover, India's economic future is simply not promising. Although the Indian government expects some decline in the birth rate, the effect of this decline will be years in coming, and in the meantime there is every reason to believe that short of massive amounts of foreign aid the present distressing economic trend—annual increases in national and per capita output but at a diminishing rate of increase—will continue.[15] Even the short-range outlook is far from promising, with large supplies of foreign grain unable to stem the rising tide of famine.

Nevertheless, India's economic demands and expectations are such that the country has every incentive to pursue an elaborate atomic energy program. Such a program brings in its wake the capacity to develop an atomic device at small cost. But to move beyond a crude atomic weapon until India's sputtering economy substantially improves—something that will probably take at least a decade—will require more resources than India can commit without jeopardizing the country's economic future.

Technologically, India has adequate manpower resources to service its present power program, and is developing a scientific manpower pool fast enough to keep pace with its ambitious atomic power schedule. The availability of the necessary skills to develop a weapons program is another matter. India does not seem to have the manpower resources in metallurgy, electronics, and nucleonics to support a sophisticated weapons program of the French variety. It might be noted in this connection that in spite of a major effort, stemming in part from national embarassment, India has thus far been unable to develop a jet engine for its HF-24 supersonic fighter bomber.

A major factor in the Indian national debate over nuclear weapons has been the psychological and political question of India's status as a great power. Plagued by uncertainties over the intentions of Communist China and humiliated by the military debacle of 1962, India clearly feels threatened by an emerging nuclear power. As one Indian writer expressed it: ". . . strong expansionist power, entrenched in Tibet, holds in its hands a loaded pistol pointed at the heart of India."[16] The pistol is also pointed at the heart of India's prestige and status as a major Asian power. This sense of loss of prestige at the hands of the Chinese may, in the long run, prove to be an overpowering stimulus to the Indians to develop their own program.

One imposing barrier to an Indian nuclear weapons program is showing every sign of crumbling as India moves in the post Gandhi/Nehru period: This is the barrier of a national abhorrence to nuclear weapons. For many years India's long-standing crusade against nuclear weapons and for the development of disarmament controls gave the Indian Government a persuasive claim on the leadership of the un-committed world, most of whose members seemed to share India's views on atomic weapons and applauded India's leadership in the fight against such weapons. Recent events in India have shown, how-ever, that the permanence of India's aversion to nuclear weapons should not be taken for granted. The death of Nehru, the humiliating military defeats of October–November, 1962, a growing sense of international isolation and impotence, and the rise of Communist China have all shaken India's national self-confidence. Myron Weiner, an American scholar long familiar with India, has noted that ". . . among the country's educated classes there is a growing sense of purposelessness, cynicism, and, most destructive of all for a country's modern sector, a sense of national incompetence."[17] An Indian newspaper was more outspoken: "The tragedy is, nobody dares to say that we are worshiping at the altar of the god that failed."[18] This psychological uneasiness, this sense that if one "god has failed"—that of nonalignment and friendliness to all nations as the best guarantees of peace—then perhaps Indians should acknowledge that another god—that of total hostility to the idea of Indian nuclear weapons—has also failed and acknowledge it before the Chinese nuclear program establishes a lead that Indians cannot overcome. This is the dilemma facing Mr. Nehru's successors. National attitudes toward nuclear weapons are being undermined by the uncomfortable and disheartening international circumstances in which India finds herself.

As the Chinese press on with their nuclear program the Indians have become increasingly less confident in India's choice of non-alignment and moral leadership as the symbols of India's power and prestige in Asia. Many Indians suspect that nuclear arms are fast becoming the most virile symbols of the new Asian power.

On the technical level there remains the issue of what sort of nuclear capability against potential enemies India could develop over the next ten years. With regard to China, India would face severe strategic problems in building a credible nuclear striking force. For example, one of India's major industrial areas, which includes the cities of Delhi, Bengal, and Jamshedpur, is close enough to China's

Tibetan bases that a short-range Chinese missile or even a medium-range bomber would be enough to threaten the Indian cities in the plains below. On the other hand, for India to mount a similar threat against Chinese cities would require at least a medium-range ballistic missile or a sophisticated aircraft resigned to a one-way mission. Thus, in order to go beyond the capability of closing passes in the Himalayas or simply a demonstration device India must, for reasons of prestige, develop a program comparable to the French effort. To do this is certainly beyond India's domestic abilities at least for the next ten years. India is faced with the problem that if it enters the nuclear race with China without foreign assistance the Indians will not be able to build what they need.

It is against this background of India's special circumstances that one must examine India's attitude toward a non-proliferation treaty. The position on a non-proliferation agreement taken, and particularly the rhetoric used, by the Indian delegation at the recent sessions of the Eighteen Nation Committee on Disarmament have been both disturbing and baffling to Americans. The United States has become accustomed to Indians taking the role in international forums of a moderator between East and West. In Geneva, however, the Indians have been acid in their choice of language—references to Western "pious preambular platitudes" and "insubstantial incantations"—and tenacious in the defense of their position. The reason for this change in Indian attitudes is not a matter of personalities, but is the result of India's new role as defender of the rights of the non-nuclear powers. The basic position the Indians have taken on the non-proliferation treaty, however, is entirely consistent with India's "peculiar circumstances."

First, the Indians vigorously object to the kind of non-proliferation treaty most desired by the nuclear powers—that is, a treaty which simply imposes restraints on the non-nuclear powers without committing the nuclear powers to specific actions. India will not sign such an important act of nuclear self-denial as a non-proliferation treaty without compensating commitments on the part of the nuclear powers. Ideally, India's stature as a nation and its national security would be best served if India were to detonate a domestic nuclear device for peaceful purposes—such as the excavation of a harbor or clearing of a mountain pass—before *both* India *and* China signed a non-proliferation agreement. India knows that there is no chance that China will sign a non-proliferation treaty; but there may be a chance to detonate a peaceful nuclear device and also gain what Foreign Minister Chagla calls a ". . . credible guarantee for our security." The pattern of Indian demands is entirely consistent with such objectives.

At Geneva and New York the Indians have pressed very hard, both alone and in concert with many of the nonaligned nations, to make the point that the only workable and acceptable treaty is one that embodies "an acceptable balance of mutual responsibilities and obligations of the nuclear and non-nuclear powers." Some mutual responsibilities and obligations of the non-nuclear powers are "mutually" agreeable, namely that no state will transfer nuclear weapons and weapons technology to any other state, and that no state will receive weapons and weapons technology from any other state. India has every reason to support this proposition even without a Chinese signature. India has the resources to develop a limited nuclear weapons capability and needs no help to reach this first stage. Therefore, at least over the short run, India is in somewhat the same position as an established nuclear power on the transfer issue—i.e., the less the better. As for the future, India would almost certainly want an automatic review clause to the treaty, or preferably a time limitation on the duration of any non-proliferation treaty. In their draft treaty of January 18, 1968 the Soviet Union and the United States have provided for a review of the treaty after 25 years "to decide whether the Treaty shall continue in force indefinitely" (Article X). This provision probably will not be acceptable to the Indians. Five or ten years from now India may want to have the benefit of the nuclear weapons technology of other countries if the Chinese threat remains persistent and the only counter is a sophisticated nuclear weapons force along the lines of the *force de frappe*.

However, when the issue of mutual responsibilities and obligations turns from the transfer problem to nuclear weapons stockpiles—what the Indians call vertical proliferation—the Indians insist that the major powers commit themselves to specific programs of reduction or, at minimum, a freeze at present weapons levels. How serious the Indians are about this is another matter. One suspects this is a bargaining position for leverage on other more practical demands. Nevertheless, the Indians may feel that if any progress is made in restraining the nuclear powers who actually sign the treaty, then these powers will be more interested in pressuring China to limit its program.

In the last analysis, India will probably be very firm on two points regarding a non-proliferation treaty. First, insistence on the right of what the Indians call "civil nuclear powers" (i.e., India) to undertake "peaceful explosions purely for their economic development even if such peaceful pursuits take place under international supervision."[19]

The Indian position here is a simple one. The Indian Government recognizes the validity of the American contention that peaceful nuclear explosions and the explosion of a nuclear weapons device are technologically indistinguishable. Nevertheless, India contends that the skills and knowledge that come from a program of using nuclear explosives are essential to the unrestricted development of this new form of energy. India is quite prepared to accept international supervision and safeguards—on the condition that these safeguards apply equally to all nations—but India must have the right to conduct its own programs. This is directly counter to the American and Soviet position that the established powers will retain control of the nuclear explosive device but, on a contract basis, will go into a country and, at a price well below development costs, use these explosives for peaceful purposes, such as the construction of harbors. India, like many other countries such as Brazil and West Germany, has complained that such arrangements, while it would get the job done, would deprive the smaller country of a vital stimulus to its own nuclear industry. India will be hard to move on this point not only for commercial reasons but because this position is consistent with India's awareness that a program including domestic nuclear explosions would give India much of the prestige China has won with its weapons program—but, in the Indian case, at far less cost and with none of the onus of becoming a nuclear weapons country.

Second, the central piece of India's position with regard to signing a non-proliferation treaty is the insistence on some form of security guarantee. When asked if India would stand by its reservations to the treaty—disarmament measures and right to the use of national nuclear explosives—Foreign Minister Chagla replied:

> We have to distinguish between the question of security and provisions of this treaty. Security is a matter apart from the question of

whether provisions of the treaty are satisfactory or not and are in conformity with the United Nations' resolution or not.[20]

From this and other indications India will probably insist that any non-proliferation treaty include provisions for the use of nuclear explosives by the so-called non-nuclear powers while simultaneously pushing for promises of specific actions on disarmament from the nuclear powers. Outside the framework of the treaty, however, India will probably levy as a condition of Indian participation security guarantees from either the United States or the Soviet Union—or preferably both.

How credible the Indians would find the kind of vague security guarantee the United States or the Soviets would be prepared to offer is another matter. Certainly the United States, and probably the Soviet Union, would not be prepared to go any further than agreeing that if India is threatened with *nuclear* blackmail or is actually attacked with *nuclear* weapons, the United States or the Soviet Union would take the matter to the Security Council and then take whatever steps they believe necessary to meet their obligations.

It is quite possible that India would be prepared to accept such an arrangement if it were coupled with language permitting some form of nuclear explosives program. First, the problems of *not* signing a non-proliferation treaty, particularly if a nuclear explosives clause were included, would be difficult for India. Second, the United States, after making such a gesture, would feel little hesitation at bringing every pressure to bear. Third, the protective mantle of the great powers without the burden of an alliance relationship would be a deterrent to China without compromising India's long-standing insistence on a position of moral and military distance from the former "colonialists."

In sum, India truly has the "peculiar circumstances" Foreign Minister Chagla referred to, and adjustments to these circumstances are as special as the circumstances themselves. One suspects that the tailoring and trimming the United States and the Soviet Union may have to do to get the Indians into a non-proliferation treaty will raise the question on whether we may be creating more potential political and security problems than we are solving by a non-proliferation treaty.

Japan

In technical terms, Japan has all the prerequisites to engineer and build advanced power reactors and to design and produce delivery systems ranging from advanced aircraft to ballistic missiles. It is surprising then that Japan, with an atomic power goal of 1,000 MWe by 1970, 9,000 by 1980, has faltered badly in its power program. Domestic reactors are hardly beyond the planning stage, while Japan's only significant advanced power station, a 166 MWe plant at Tokai Mura, was imported from Great Britain.[21] This contrast between a clear capacity to produce weapons-grade fissionable material and fabricate an atomic device, and what seems to be a reluctance to move even to a point where Japan would have the option to build nuclear weapons in a short period of time is best understood in terms of Japan's national circumstances.

Japan's physical circumstances present a major disincentive to acquiring or building nuclear weapons. Small, insular, and densely populated, Japan has no sites for atmospheric testing and would be hard pressed to find suitable underground sites. The very density of the population and the concentration of industrial centers not only raise the probability of massive damage from nuclear attack but preclude the dispersal of nuclear weapons so necessary to a credible deterrent. Furthermore, Japan's insular position lifts the threat of a ground attack such as India faces and thereby the attraction of tactical nuclear weapons.

From the standpoint of economic strength and technological skills, however, Japan's capacity is roughly equivalent to that of France; and there is no reason why the Japanese, if they should so decide, could not duplicate the French program. The population level is stable, and technical skills and industrial capacity show every sign of continuing to develop, although periodic recessions may cut into the remarkable increases in GNP which have averaged 8% over the past few years. Another incentive for developing an atomic program on the scale of the Indian effort is Japan's power needs. Japan's present and potential supplies of hydro-electric and fossil fuel sources will not be adequate if Japan is to continue to grow at its present rate.

The Japanese, unlike the Indians, do not feel threatened by the

Chinese bomb and seem convinced that the existence of Chinese nuclear weapons will not significantly affect the balance of military power in the Far East. This confidence is in part the result of Japan's geographic circumstances, in part the result of Japan's sense of security because of its place in the American defense system, and in part the fact that Japan has grown accustomed to the idea of nuclear weapons in its part of the world. The Japanese probably also feel that the efforts they are making to develop closer political and economic ties with China will build a mutual sense of confidence and trust, thereby giving the Chinese less reason to misbehave in their Japanese relations. For all these reasons, then, there is little incentive for the Japanese to want nuclear weapons because of any sense of external threat.

An important factor in the Japanese calculations with regard to nuclear weapons is Japan's present reliance on the United States for military protection. Since September, 1951, when the United States signed a peace treaty with Japan ending the occupation, the Japanese have maintained a mutual security treaty with the United States which permits United States military bases in Japan. For all practical purposes Japan is part of the American Far Eastern alliance network. Japan is also committed to permit United States forces in Japan until at least 1971. In the sense that "aligned" is used in this study, Japan is unquestionably aligned with a nuclear power. As a consequence, the Japanese have additional reason to suppress the nuclear urge. With the presence of American forces in Japan as testimony, the United States has in effect given Japan the same sort of nuclear guarantee that we have given the NATO countries. Japan's apparent satisfaction with this arrangement of placing the nuclear defense of the country in the hands of the United States represents a major disincentive to acquiring nuclear weapons.

There are also important psychological and legal circumstances affecting Japanese attitudes toward nuclear weapons. One has only to recall the deep emotions stirred in Japan on the occasion of the 20th anniversary of the Hiroshima bombing or to read a few of the moving accounts of the death agonies of Japan's atomic victims to draw some measure of Japan's national hostility to atomic weapons and their "death ash."[22] Such incidents as the *Fukuryu Maru* accident in 1954, when a Japanese fishing boat was contaminated by the nuclear fallout of an American explosion, and such statistics as those of the Japanese government that in 1959 there were over two hundred thousand Japanese who sought help because of atomic disease, have served to keep alive the Japanese national antipathy toward atomic weapons.[23]

The late Hayato Ikedo, who was Prime Minister of Japan in 1962, wrote a letter to N. S. Khrushchev protesting the Soviet Union's 1961 decision to resume atmospheric testing and expressing what is to this day the Japanese national consensus on nuclear weapons:

> To [the] Japanese, the only people who have experienced the horrors of atomic explosions, the utilization of nuclear energy for military purposes is absolutely intolerable. . . . I am convinced it is the paramount responsibility we Japanese owe to history and mankind to appeal unremittingly in order to see that the tragedy we have experienced is never again repeated on earth.[24]

One of the reasons why Japanese national attitudes are so profoundly hostile to the acquisition of nuclear weapons is rooted in what seems to be a basic transformation of the character of Japanese society since 1945. In 1947 General Douglas MacArthur described this transformation and attributed the change in large part to the results of the American occupation.

> We have demobilized the troops, demilitarized the country, torn down military installations. Psychologically, I believe the success has been equally propitious. . . . Japan understands as thoroughly as any nation that war does not pay. Her spiritual revolution has been probably the greatest the world has ever known. . . . I believe sincerely and absolutely that it is here to stay. . . . The Japanese are relying upon the spirituality of the world to protect them against undue aggression.[25]

To a certain extent MacArthur was correct. The traditional prestige of the Japanese military class was shattered in 1945 and there seems to be little chance of its recovery over at least the next decade. In its place there is a new pacifism and individualism in Japanese society which has contributed to the gradual destruction of many of the traditional citadels of authority.[26]

One practical result of this process of social transformation which includes such strong elements of pacifism is the existence of the famous Article IX of the Japanese Constitution of 1947, the so-called "war renunciation" clause, which imposes stringent limitations on Japanese rearmament. Other results include a total subjection of the military to civilian authority and what one student of Japan has called an "inward looking nationalism," where the Japanese pride themselves not on international political and military successes but on the vitality of their economy and the success of their athletes.[27]

Taken together, this combination of psychological, legal, and social restraints raises an impressive barrier to Japanese interest in nuclear weapons.

If this strong array of disincentives could somehow be put aside, Japan could comfortably develop the long-range strategic bombers necessary to have a "nuclear capability" against China. Moreover, if Chinese defensive capabilities should improve, it is also likely that Japan would be able to maintain the pace by developing medium-range ballistic missiles. Over the longer range, however, Japan does not have the resources or physical circumstances to match China in a nuclear weapons race—and this discrepancy in potential might serve as a deterrent to Japanese interest in nuclear weapons.

The 1947 constitution, which permits the Japanese defense establishment to develop or accept only those weapons which are necessary to defend the country against aggression, also has had its limiting effect on Japan's potential nuclear capability. In keeping with the constitution, Japan has limited its aircraft development to the domestic production of aircraft such as the American F-104J fighter-interceptor built in Japan under contract. On the other hand, Japan has plans for the construction of missile sites for the eventual installation of Nike-Ajax surface-to-air missiles. The skills acquired in developing these projects would be an important asset in any future strategic weapons program. Moreover, in the field of rocketry Japan's legal restrictions are not as limiting as those in West Germany, where the West Germans are prohibited from domestic manufacture of "long-range missiles and guided missiles." The definition of such missiles—". . . missiles such that the speed or direction of motion can be influenced after the instant of launching by a mechanism inside or outside the missile . . ."—puts Germany, for example, completely out of the communications satellite business unless the rocket is manufactured outside the country or the Germans participate in bilateral or international programs. For their part, the Japanese have no such restrictions on their technology and will, for example, soon send into orbit their own satellites. Once Japan has developed the skills to sustain a space program, the ability to develop missiles will come as a natural bonus.

Although Japan has the capacity to rival France in the nuclear field, there is little doubt that any Japanese incentives to press for a nuclear weapons program—such as the stimulus it would give to the economy—are clearly outweighed by the restraints imposed by the country's physical circumstances, its relationship to the United States, and to its national psychology. As in the case of India, the important national circumstances that give rise to Japan's position on nuclear weapons are highly individualistic. While the Japanese have some of the same "kinds" of problems as India, the differences in intensity overshadow the similarities in form.

Despite the formidable barriers to a weapons program, Japan's present policy of self-denial is not immutable. Although the accumulation of Chinese nuclear successes has not yet convinced the Japanese that they must have their own weapons program, there are increasing indications that Japan intends to keep its nuclear options open.

In 1965, a year after the first Chinese nuclear explosion, the Japanese Government officially took the position that if it could be demonstrated that some form of nuclear weapons was purely "defensive," then the constitutional prohibitions on nuclear weapons would not be applicable.[28] Moreover, throughout the last months of 1966 and into 1967 the Japanese have moved closer to the Indian position on security measures to protect non-nuclear powers and the Indian contention that the nuclear powers must agree to specific disarmament obligations in any non-proliferation pact.

On the first point, that of the collective security of the non-nuclear powers, the Japanese, already enjoying the protection of the existing American-Japanese security arrangement, have not been as outspoken and demanding as the Indians. Foreign Minister Takeo Miki stated in March of 1967 that a collective security guarantee against nuclear attack "was a matter of crucial importance" and recommended that "all non-nuclear nations be guaranteed for collective security by a United Nations resolution."[29] This and other statements by Japanese leaders seem intended not to encourage new security guarantees if a treaty should be agreed to, but to convince the Japanese that a continuation of present arrangements with the United States is vital if Japan is to avoid a national nuclear weapons program. On the question of the obligations of the nuclear powers, Foreign Minister Miki told the Japanese: "As long as the purpose of this treaty is the elimination of anxiety which would be cast upon mankind by the proliferation of nuclear weapons, it is not enough that the treaty prevent the proliferation of nuclear weapons among countries which do not possess them; it should go further to make clear the sincere intention on the part of the countries which possess nuclear weapons to make efforts toward nuclear disarmament, leading ultimately to general disarmament. It is true that disarmament cannot be achieved at once, but concrete measures should be taken with a view to realizing step by step the fervent desire of mankind that nuclear weapons should be abolished. Otherwise the Treaty would lose its moral foundation."[30]

Where the United States will have the most difficult time with Japan, however, is over the question of the peaceful uses of atomic energy. Japan has joined West Germany and India in demanding that any non-proliferation agreement should not discriminate against the nuclear have-nots in the commercial uses of atomic energy. In mounting a campaign against the nuclear powers and their determination to retain control of nuclear devices, the Japanese have formed an informal but active partnership with the West Germans. Both these nations have observer missions at Geneva, where the lobbying must necessarily be done in cooperation with like-minded nations represented on the Eighteen Nation Disarmament Conference such as India and Brazil.

With the Japanese parliament, the Government of Japan has taken the position that while Japan has "no intention at this time to develop nuclear explosive devices . . . our future generations should not be deprived of the opportunity to take part in the progress of atomic science."[31] There is no doubt that the Japanese business community as well as the defense and foreign ministry are solidly behind this demand that Japan's future commercial (and fortuitously military) interests be protected. The suggestion of Foreign Minister Miki that a non-proliferation treaty should have a definite period of validity—five years was mentioned—is consistent with Japan's increasing hesitation to sign an open-ended treaty.

As for the future, the nuclear powers cannot take it for granted that Japan, with its highly individualistic views of the advantages and disadvantages of a non-proliferation treaty—as opposed to a non-proliferation policy—will sign a treaty that does not give full consideration to Japan's demands.

West Germany

Of all the problems arising from the spread of nuclear weapons, none has caused the United States more anguish than the "German problem." And no problem better illustrates the dangers of devising universal laws of behavior as a guide to policy.

Because it is now both economically and technologically feasible for Europeans to think about developing their own nuclear weapons program, it is only natural that there are differences within the Alliance over ownership and use of nuclear weapons. At the root of the problem is European awareness that there may be alternatives to complete dependence on the United States to deter the Soviet nuclear threat to Europe.

The United States has taken the position that, although the requirement for nuclear defense of Europe is fully met by our own strategic forces, we appreciate the problems of European political confidence caused by the ultimate U.S. control of NATO's nuclear forces. Consequently, we have sought in consultation with our Allies to devise a means of meeting the "need" of Europeans for a share in control to dampen European interest in independent nuclear forces, eliminate the need for further "two-key" or bilateral nuclear weapons arrangements, and—in more recent plans—avoid the political and military disadvantages of deploying nuclear missiles on the continent of Europe. As to the last objective, it should be noted that there is little enthusiasm anywhere for land-based missiles in "their" country.

The various multilateral schemes considered by the United States, such as the MLF, were attempts to fulfill the objectives of sharing nuclear control while discouraging national nuclear efforts. The plan's backers also hoped to help create a framework or model of Atlantic partnership which could be of major importance to the future of

European unity. The latest and best known such scheme, the MLF (Multilateral Force) was designed also to avoid putting strategic missiles in Europe.

In the public mind, however, the collective European nuclear force concept, such as the ill-fated MLF project, is designed primarily to meet German aspirations to play a greater role in the nuclear affairs of the Alliance. This identification was stimulated not only by the press but by the public and private concern of many United States officials that Germany will follow France along the path to a national nuclear force if its energies, ambitions, and finances are not channeled into a collective force. The sense of urgency caused attention to concentrate on this issue rather than on the more fundamental problem of how best to give Europeans a voice in deterring the Soviet MRBM threat to Europe. Consequently, although no multilateral force is now under active consideration, any talk of nuclear sharing still immediately turns to the issue of Germany and nuclear weapons, eliciting reactions varying from uneasiness to near pathological fulminations. Memories of German oppression are too tender and distrust of the German national character is too widespread to permit rational discussion of nuclear sharing within the Alliance if that discussion begins with a plea for German nuclear "equality."

Nevertheless, German and American officials who still insist on the urgency of somehow enlarging the German role in the nuclear field are apparently prepared to pay the political costs of a program of nuclear sharing advertised as a means of giving the Germans nuclear equality within the Alliance. These costs would include: increased French hostility, the risk that the Soviets would shatter whatever hopes remain that German reunification can be achieved, and the prospect that the East European countries now in a process of political and economic diversification would consolidate in the face of a German nuclear threat. Much of this reaction could be expected whatever form increased German participation took, but the United States' pressure for rapid solution and concentration on the purely German aspect of the larger problem of the nuclear defense of Europe are guaranteed to intensify and exacerbate the reaction.

West Germany's economic resurgence and evidence of growing political confidence, it is argued, indicate that Germany cannot be forever denied what nations of lesser stature can now obtain. Hence the United States and the "honest Germans" should move swiftly to give Germany a measure of nuclear participation before the forces of latent German militarism demand a national nuclear force *à la française*. Moreover, the argument goes, West Germany, as the most exposed country in Western Europe, is in the uncomfortable position of having to depend totally on the United States nuclear deterrent for its defense. Therefore, West Germans are particularly vulnerable to the Gaullist argument that the United States will not expose its own cities to nuclear destruction for the sake of Germany. As for the physical presence of some 200,000 American troops in Germany, these "hostages" to American fidelity could be withdrawn at any time.

F. W. Mulley, a British expert on defense issues and now Minister of State for Europe, wrote in 1962:

> One may deplore the risks attendant upon a proliferation of nuclear powers but it is hardly surprising that France, for example, is seeking to join the nuclear club for reasons of prestige and in order to exert greater influence upon the affairs of the alliance. All of the arguments which led Britain to decide to develop her own nuclear weapons are equally valid from the French point of view for France herself, and *there is no reason why other members of NATO should not decide to follow suit.*[32]

The logic of this argument has been compelling, particularly to Washington. The specter of a West Germany with an independent nuclear force apparently has so disturbed Washington that it has hardly been questioned whether the French or British experience has in fact any relevance for Germany. It is perhaps time that this question be asked.

To be sure, West German advances in nuclear technology since 1958 have been impressive and help create the impression that the Germans are laying the foundation for a weapons program. Notable accomplishments in recent years include a program of nine power reactors scheduled for completion by 1969—including a 237-megawatt plant at Gundremmingen—a fuel fabrication plant, and a national investment in atomic energy programs that is now running over $200 million a year. In the ultracentrifuge field, German scientists were among the pioneers. However, little has been heard about

German activity in this field since October, 1960, when it was announced—amid a flurry of newspaper comment—that henceforth the
work would be classified.

The composite picture of West German prospects in the nuclear
field is therefore one of increasing strength and diversity. In a very
few years, if present plans are carried out, West Germany will not
only become one of the leading commercial competitors in the nuclear field but will have the capacity to build a bomb in a very
short time, and at little cost. But to say that Germany has a strong
chance to become a leader in the nuclear power field is clearly not
the same as saying that the Germans will press on to nuclear weapons if the United States fails to discover some way of sublimating
this very natural drive. A look at West Germany's national circumstances may help to show this.

On the incentive side of the ledger, it is true that Germany
would be in an extremely dangerous position if it were forced to
defend itself against the Soviet Union with conventional arms alone.
The vast open northern plain which carried German armies into
Russia can also serve as a gateway for the Russians into West Germany. Because West Germany, either alone or even in concert with
its Allies, could not hope to block this channel with conventional
arms for very long the incentive to acquire an assured nuclear-
weapons defense is very high.

On the other hand, although West Germany is a large country
by European standards, with a decentralized industrial and population pattern, its physical circumstances are not favorable for a nuclear weapons program. Adequate underground testing sites would be
difficult to find, and the country is too small and crowded to satisfy
the requirements for dispersal of a fixed missile system. And though
West Germany has the technological and economic base to duplicate the nuclear weapons programs of France and Great Britain,
does it have the political incentives?

Alone among the major powers in Europe, West Germany is a
nation with a strong sense of national grievance. The reunification
issue has a direct bearing on Bonn's position on the acquisition of
nuclear weapons, as Foreign Minister Gerhard Schröder indicated in
July, 1965, when he stated that West Germany was not prepared to
renounce the acquisition of nuclear weapons until the Soviet Union

consented to the reunification of Germany. He thus brought into sharp focus a major German incentive for creating the option of acquiring a nuclear capability but also for refraining from doing so. For the usefulness of the nuclear weapons issue in gaining reunification would almost certainly be shattered once Germany actually acquired weapons.

It is at this point that comparison with France breaks down. President de Gaulle needed nuclear weapons in being to pursue his objective of reasserting French influence on the Continent; Germany needs the threat of acquiring nuclear weapons to force progress on reunification. West Germany has serious reservations about the non-proliferation agreement not because it wants nuclear weapons but because the Germans do not want to be deprived of the threat of acquiring them.

To look at the other side of the coin for a moment, suppose West Germany did actually decide to build a nuclear force. If it were to be more than just a prestige symbol, if it were designed actually to threaten the Soviet Union, it would run a high risk of drawing a Soviet attack while still in the development stage. Few countries would have a more precarious ride to a nuclear capability than West Germany, exposed as it would be to a pre-emptive Soviet strike. At the moment it has five heavy fighter-bomber squadrons of Lockheed F-104's which could be used as delivery vehicles, but their chances of success against Soviet defenses would be very low indeed. West Germany would have to make a great investment in armaments even to come up to the standard of France's present nuclear force.

In summary, Germany's incentives to develop an independent nuclear force are clearly outweighed by the restraints imposed by its special circumstances. But this conclusion rests precariously on a structure of assumptions: that German policy will be rational; that our commitment to defend West Germany will retain some credibility; and that we will not sacrifice German reunification for an accommodation with the Soviet Union. Under these conditions, the Germans are not likely to want their own nuclear weapons, for they are surely aware that nothing would so permanently solidify the division of Germany. What they do want is the bargaining power that the *threat* of acquiring nuclear weapons may give them.

Given its peculiar national problems, it is no wonder that West Germany would be most thankful if the non-proliferation treaty were to be quietly shelved. The non-proliferation issue poses difficult problems for the Germans both internally because the Germans are not of one mind on the issue, and externally because the Germans simply do not have the option to refuse to sign a non-proliferation treaty once it is agreed to by the negotiating parties. No state likes to be in such a position, particularly when, no matter what form the final draft takes, Germany will have sacrificed the nuclear weapons option without any increase in security commitments, or promise of progress on the reunification issue.

Important sectors of West German political life would certainly not agree with the above analysis of Germany's stake in a non-proliferation treaty. Most Social Democrats and Free Democrats would argue that a further pledge that West Germany will never arm with nuclear weapons would accelerate Germany's recent small successes in "building bridges" to the East. This group feels that the resistance of the Foreign and Defense Minister and the Christian Democratic party to a non-proliferation treaty is damaging the so-called Ostpolitik of detente with Eastern Europe and the Soviet Union. These advocates of the permanent renunciation of German access to nuclear weapons will take small comfort in the recent publication of the memoirs of Hans Kroll, West Germany's long-time Ambassador to the Soviet Union. Kroll writes that the Russians were prepared in 1958 to exchange negotiations for a peace treaty leading to a reunification of Germany for an ironclad pledge from Germany that the Germans permanently renounce nuclear weapons. Kroll says this idea was killed by the United States Government. Some Germans will now point out that Germany is now being asked to make the same pledge for nothing.

As the negotiations proceed, West Germany will continue to operate deprived of the option of actually refusing to sign a treaty agreed to by the Soviet Union and the United States. The West German Government finds itself in the awkward position of trying to resolve its own internal arguments over the non-proliferation concept while simultaneously trying to defend West Germany's long range interests without indicating what is really bothering Germany. As a result, the West Germans have concentrated on the technological handicaps a non-proliferation treaty might impose on West Germany's burgeoning atomic energy program. The German position here is being defended with vigor and intelligence by Willy Brandt, the Social Democratic Foreign Minister, which is an important indication of the general reluctance within West Germany to sign the treaty envisioned by the United States. The Social Democrats are in the difficult position of trying to mediate in a dispute that never would have arisen if the United States had not made a non-proliferation treaty one of the most important objectives of our foreign policy.

In what is certainly the most convincing and fair-minded appraisal of West German attitudes on the non-proliferation issue, Theo Sommer, Foreign Editor of *Die Zeit*, observed in a recent study of the proliferation question that "no international problem of recent years has been more consistently misstated, misunderstood, or willfully misrepresented than that of West Germany's nuclear policy." [33] Mr. Sommer argues that this situation can largely be attributed to the failure of the West German Government to state its case with candor and conviction. This is certainly true. But it is also true that the United States in its relentless pursuit of a universal remedy to a problem that seems to defy universal solutions has failed to attempt to understand the "German problem." And in this failure has sown seeds for years of strain and uncertainty in our relations with West Germany.

Israel

Israel is a prime example of a country where standard technical and economic indices of capability to build nuclear weapons are largely irrelevant in analyzing intentions. In Israel's case geographic conditions and the overall political-diplomatic context of her position in the Middle East govern the decision to go nuclear. Moreover, the dramatic change in Israel's geo-political position brought on by the recent Arab-Israeli war not only underlines this point but will undoubtedly have a profound influence on Israel's defense policy, including attitudes toward the possession of nuclear weapons.

Even before the 1967 war changed the terms of reference in the Middle East, the prospect of an Israeli nuclear weapons program had always made Israel's friends almost as nervous as it had her enemies. Late in 1960 press reports of the construction of a secret nuclear installation in Israel were finally confirmed by the Israeli Government. This installation, which went into operation in 1965, was built with the help of French scientists and equipment, and is located in

Dimona, which lies halfway between Beersheba and Sodom in the Negev Desert. Built to a capacity of 24,000 kilowatts, this natural uranium, heavy-water moderated type reactor is capable of producing sufficient fissionable material for about one small atomic bomb per year. The discovery of the Dimona reactor naturally caused a mild international uproar. This reaction ensued not only because of the secrecy under which the Dimona reactor was constructed but because of the dire predictions of what the introduction of nuclear weapons into the tinder box of the Middle East would mean.

Premier David Ben Gurion, in explaining the Dimona project to the Israeli Knesset (parliament) after the press disclosure, described the installation as ". . . a scientific institute for research in problems of arid zones and desert flora and fauna." He also characterized reports that an Israeli atomic bomb was under construction as ". . . either a deliberate or an unconscious untruth."[34] Since that time Ben Gurion's successor, Prime Minister Levi Eshkol, has repeatedly stated Israel's position on nuclear weapons: "Israel will not be the first country to introduce nuclear weapons into the Middle East."

President Kennedy was so disturbed by the secrecy of the Dimona project and the implications of the introduction of nuclear weapons into the Middle East that he pressed Ben Gurion very hard to place Dimona under safeguards. Ben Gurion and his successor have consistently refused to permit such inspections. Nevertheless, there has been speculation in the press that the United States has worked out an arrangement with Israel whereby American engineers from the Atomic Energy Commission conduct informal, unpublished annual inspections. If there is such an arrangement, it would have the double advantage for Israel of reassuring the United States that Israel is not producing an atomic bomb while simultaneously keeping the Arab states in a state of constant uncertainty as to whether Israel is picking up her undisputed nuclear option.

In Israel's continuing assessment of its national position on nuclear weapons, geographical considerations play perhaps the largest role. This is as true for the development of nuclear weapons as well as for their usefulness in Israel's offensive and defensive strategy. For example, until the recent war Israel's geographic circumstances posed a strong disincentive to the actual development of a national nuclear force. From Israel's northern border with Lebanon to its southern border on the Gulf of Aqaba was a distance of some 260 miles. The country's width ranged from a few miles near Tel Aviv to a maximum of around seventy miles south of Beersheba in the Negev. Consequently, an atmospheric test was clearly out of the question except at, say, a French site; and underground testing, while practical and permissible under the test ban, would have been dangerous if venting occurred.

Israel had, and still has, another physical disincentive when it comes to the question of introducing nuclear weapons into the area. Although Israel's government has tried with some success to decentralize the country's population and industry, the fact remains that Israel remains highly vulnerable to massive damage from only a few nuclear weapons. Of the country's some two million inhabitants, some four hundred thousand live in the Tel Aviv/Jerusalem area. Thus, the coastal area of about 120 miles from the Lebanon border to the Gaza strip has the bulk of the country's population and industry. This high degree of centralization is a clear disincentive to entering the nuclear weapons arena where space is such an advantage.

Israel's geographic circumstances also play the dominant role in the determination of the country's military strategy. Until Israel acquired the West Bank of the Jordan, the Syrian heights overlooking the northeast border, and the Sinai desert, Israel's best defense against attack was the use of her tight inner lines of communication and supply. In a matter of a few hours troops and supplies could be moved from one border to another. Operating from this central core of communications and supplies and faced with the threat of a converging Arab attack on a small area, Israel relied on punitive counterthrusts to Arab probes and a preemptive blitzkrieg with conventional weapons as the foundation of her defense strategy. In such an offensive strategy nuclear weapons were of little consequence. Now, as a result of Israel's 1966 successes, the Israel defense policy may have to be drastically overhauled. And with this change, nuclear weapons may come to play an important role.

Assuming a peace settlement is not reached in the Middle East and Israel retains at least the West Bank and possibly the Sinai, Israel's security from attack will certainly be enhanced. In the process of consolidating this increase in security, however, Israel, in order to offset the new problem of maintaining inner lines of communication and supply, may feel compelled to alter the "mix" of her defense strategy by taking up her option on nuclear weapons. This may happen even if Israel is forced by international pressure to give up its recent territorial gains without a peace settlement simply because the Israelis are realistic enough to know that the Arab forces will not forever remain inferior in conventional warfare.

Although Israel's economic circumstances are relatively unimportant in any decision to develop nuclear weapons, the country's economic problems are of a nature as to work against any decision to build nuclear weapons. Long dependent on German reparations and remittances from the American Jews to take the strain off its perennial balance of payments deficits, Israel is now facing a gradual diminishing of German reparations capital and some closing of some markets in Europe due to the Common Market at a time when the debt service burden is increasing substantially. Although the country has until recently maintained annual increases in real terms of the gross national product of around 11 percent, the rate of growth in 1966 had slowed to around 1 to 2 percent. Always faced with deficits in the current account balance of trade, this deficit stood at about $465 million in 1966.

Israel's economic problems are complicated by the fact that Israel's defense budget is not only running at around 23 percent of the total budget but, more importantly, includes the purchase of extraordinary amounts of foreign military equipment, such as Sherman tanks of American origin, British Centurian tanks, French Mystere and Mirage III jets, and American surface-to-air missiles. Mounting a conventional force powerful enough to offset Soviet equipment provided the Arabs is a difficult enough task, but to do more than detonate a crude nuclear device would impose on Israel's economy a severe strain. In purely economic terms, Israel may be forced to develop nuclear weapons, but it would be most reluctant to initiate a nuclear arms race.

On the technological front, Professor Ernst Bergmann, the director of Israel's atomic energy program until 1966, contends that Israel has enough scientists to handle a modest weapons program but as yet not enough technicians. As to Israel's progress in developing a nuclear weapons option, Professor Bergmann had the following to say about the oft-drawn distinction between a "peaceful" nuclear program and one calculated to bring a country to the threshold of nuclear weapons: "It is very important to understand that by developing atomic energy for peaceful uses, you reach the nuclear option: *there are no two atomic energies.*"[35] Important results of Israel's atomic energy program have been the development of the capability of producing heavy water and deriving uranium as a by-product of the phosphate fertilizer industry. Taken together, there is no doubt that Israel has the technological capacity to develop a modest nuclear striking force without significant outside help. The delivery to Israel of some two squadrons of United States light bombers, the A-4, ironically enough gives Israel the delivery capacity for atomic weapons that the United States has so long dreaded.

Surely the most pressing consideration—and in this case, incentive—for an Israeli weapons program is the country's sense of unrelieved external danger. As Shimon Peres, former Deputy Minister of Defense in 1963, put it:

> . . . Israel is the only country in the world—I emphasize the country and not the political system—that is in actual and professed danger of attack. . . . The Arabs are not prepared to entertain the thought of co-existence . . . they are threatening and preparing an armed attack. . . . We are confronted with prolonged hostility that has gone on for half a generation and more; we may, moreover, expect changes in the area and in the type of armaments employed therein.[36]

Confronted with a joint—if ineffectual—Arab military command which is constantly preparing for the next war and all but surrounded by enemies, Israel would have a powerful incentive to develop nuclear weapons if Tel Aviv should lose confidence in its ability to repeat the 1956 and 1967 campaigns, or if Egypt should somehow acquire nuclear weapons.

Israel could almost certainly move faster along the spectrum of nuclear capabilities than Egypt if—and this is a large if—any Egyptian nuclear striking force was based on domestically produced nuclear weapons and the delivery vehicles the U.S.S.R. has already provided. It is the uncertainty that the U.S.S.R. might go beyond this level of support and actually give the Egyptians weapons that would in the last analysis prevent Israel from initiating a nuclear weapons race with Egypt. As Shimon Peres has put it, the Egyptians have the advantages of "a greater degree of aid on the international level," "numerical superiority," and "more and better weapons." On the other side, the Israelis are able to offset these advantages with the "qualitative superiority" of their forces.[37] The introduction of nuclear weapons into the present "qualitative" vs "quantitative" equation, which now favors Israel in the employment of conventional weapons, would be to Israel's short-range disadvantage if a nuclear race began before the Arabs have closed the conventional weapons gap. Nevertheless, the acquisition of new territory with its new military problems of defending a large area combined with the incentives this same territory offers for the testing of nuclear weapons will create pressures within Israel to add a nuclear deterrent to its defense policy.

As for the future, how long will Israel remain satisfied with simply holding open the nuclear weapons option? Obviously, countering Arab hostility is the centerpiece of Israel's defense policy. The combination of retaliatory raids and, in the case of extreme national danger, preemptive offensive thrusts have worked brilliantly over the past twenty years. Israel would certainly be reluctant to abandon or modify this military strategy before the Arabs have overcome their present and seemingly intractable conventional military inferiority—and this process may take years. On the other side of the ledger Tel Aviv knows that such action would not only provoke an attack by the Arabs but probably force the Soviets to station atomic weapons in Egypt or to give the Arabs a security guarantee. Taken together, these considerations indicate that Israel's best interest continues to be a policy of holding the nuclear option open, thereby keeping the Arabs uncertain as to Tel Aviv intentions while simultaneously seeking a political settlement in the Middle East, a settlement that would make the nuclear weapons issue largely irrelevant to Israel's future. Unlike a number of other countries—notably France, China, and India—the prestige and international stature reputed to be a bonus effect of developing an atomic weapon is not an important consideration in Israel's calculations.

Israel's flexible and highly pragmatic position on the development of nuclear weapons, which is well tailored to the country's special circumstances, is now fundamentally threatened by the nonproliferation treaty. If Israel signs the agreement before a political settlement is reached in the Middle East, she will be giving up an important option prematurely. If Israel refuses to sign, the Arabs will take this refusal as proof that Israel is developing a nuclear weapon and will probably launch a preemptive attack on Israel as soon as Cairo has reconstructed its military forces. The humiliating defeats of 1956 and 1967, it should be remembered, came after the Israelis struck first. In any event, if Israel should refuse to sign a non-proliferation treaty, this action would almost certainly block the way to a political settlement in the Middle East for many years to come.

Israel's present ambiguous position on the non-proliferation treaty is an indication of Tel Aviv's dilemma when faced with this particular Hobson's choice. Foreign Minister Abba Eban has said that Israel is reserving its position on the non-proliferation treaty until a draft is available. This position is purely and simply a way of buying time until the position of the United States on guarantees becomes clear, and the neutralist countries at Geneva have had a chance to link the non-proliferation treaty with disarmament. One thing seems clear, however: if the United States is insistent on a non-proliferation treaty with an Israeli signature, Washington may have to give Israel something akin to a bilateral defense treaty. Without such a guarantee—something Israel has sought for years—Israel's short-range security would not be served by a non-proliferation treaty. And with the immediacy of the Arab threat, who can expect Israel to think ahead for more than four or five years?

To its possible surprise, then, the United States may be asked what price it is prepared to pay to bring Israel into a non-proliferation pact.

The United Arab Republic

In technical terms, the United Arab Republic's prospects of achieving a domestic nuclear weapons program are hopelessly barren. Even Denis Healey's depressing conclusion that enough guidebooks to nuclear power are now in the public domain so that "any society which is capable of producing a watch or a motor car is capable of producing a mechanism for triggering off an atomic explosion" fails to apply to Egypt. Why should we concern ourselves with President Gamal Abdel Nasser's nuclear bravado when one suspects that Egypt's ability to produce a "watch or a motor car" is highly questionable. However, the fact that Moscow, Washington,

and Tel Aviv are all concerned about the United Arab Republic
and nuclear weapons is one more illustration that a country's
political-diplomatic circumstances are far more important in determining motivations for going nuclear than technological-economic considerations. That Egypt could rate the attention it has received as a
possible nuclear contender reflects a growing awareness that even the
most technically backward can enter the nuclear weapons field if
the incentives are there.

If President Nasser should undertake a domestic nuclear weapons program he would have to find the resources outside of Egypt.
Although Egypt has increased its industrial production from $753.6
million in 1952 to over $2 billion in 1965 and raised the per capita
income from $120 to $180 in the same period, the country is simply
not equipped with the domestic industrial and technological skills
to build its own nuclear weapons. To overcome these domestic de-
ficiencies in the related field of rocketry Egypt has capitalized on the
increasing availability of an international commodity which, in time,
will destroy any meaningful correlation between possession of nuclear weapons and domestic technological levels. This commodity is
an international set of technological and scientific journeymen. Prior
to the collapse of Egyptian–West German relations in 1965, there
were more than 500 West German and other European scientists,
engineers, and technicians working in Egypt under contract on the
United Arab Republic's rocket and jet aircraft program. The most
dramatic result of this effort has been the testing of several liquid-
propellant rockets such as the single state Al Kaher (The Conqueror),
with ranges of 100 to 400 nm.

Even assuming the increasing availability of a breed of international journeymen who have nuclear weapons skills for hire, it is
far from clear that President Nasser wants nuclear weapons as well
as missiles. Technically and geographically a base is there if the decision is made. The Soviets have provided a 2-megawatt reactor built
at Inchass in northeastern Egypt. The Inchass reactor, like the Israeli
facility at Dimona, is not under United Nations safeguards. Significantly enough—and naturally enough considering the inferiority of
the United Arab Republic in the nuclear field—Nasser has offered
to place the Inchass reactor under the United Nations if Israel does
the same with Dimona.

As for Egypt's geographic circumstances bearing on the nuclear weapons question, President Nasser would have little trouble finding a place to test his atomic device, either underground or above ground. Nevertheless, despite Egypt's size, the country's physical circumstances would act as a disincentive or deterrent to the development of nuclear weapons. This is because of the high degree of population and industrial concentration along the Nile. While Egypt's vast empty expanses would be ideal for the installation of widely dispersed missiles, any sensible estimate of what two 50 kt nuclear weapons dropped on Cairo and Alexandria respectively would do to Egypt's urban population and industrial capacity is enough to underline what a major disincentive the country's physical circumstances are to introducing nuclear weapons into the area.

Granting that President Nasser can defy all the standard technological and economic indices and actually build an atomic weapon, under what circumstances would he actually do so?

President Nasser, as the avowed leader of the Arab countries, is pledged to destroy Israel. No more compelling incentive could exist for developing nuclear weapons if such weapons could wipe away the shame and humiliation of 1948, 1956, and 1967. The 1967 debacle was more personal and galling for Nasser than his earlier failure and the aftermath more threatening to his position. Consequently it could be argued that Nasser will decide that a demonstration of a nuclear weapons capacity—whether imported or domestically created with foreign technology—is necessary. Egypt is, thus, in the highly dangerous position of deriving incentives for developing nuclear weapons not only from a sense of unfulfilled national ambition but also from a sense of national insecurity. President Nasser's reaction to the 1960 rumors that Israel was developing nuclear weapons is an indication of the United Arab Republic's deep concern over nuclear weapons. Nasser said that if it were certain that Israel was constructing a bomb:

> . . . it will mean the beginning of war between us and Israel, because we cannot permit Israel to manufacture an atomic bomb. It is inevitable that we should attack the base of aggression, even if we have to mobilize four million to destroy it.[38]

Although President Nasser has repeated this threat of a preventive war many times, the only effective counter Egypt has at the moment is the shield of the Soviet Union. After the Soviet Union's experience with China it is unlikely that the Russians will provide Egypt with enough technological assistance to allow the Egyptians to reach the threshold of a nuclear weapons capability. Moscow has been burned badly by assisting a weapons program and then losing control of the beneficiary; Kosygin will hardly wish to repeat this experience with the highly unstable United Arab Republic. Consistent with this limitation on Soviet technological aid is the reported refusal of the Soviets in late 1965 to sell Egypt nuclear weapons. This refusal apparently came at the time of a visit of Marshal Grechko, the Soviet Union's recently appointed Defense Minister, when the Marshal led a high-powered Soviet military delegation to Cairo in December of 1965. The Soviets clearly have no reason to give the United Arab Republic an independent nuclear weapons capability; and given Soviet attitudes toward nuclear weapons sharing arrangements within the Warsaw Pact there is no reason to believe that Nasser will be offered a sharing scheme.

Because of the delicacy of the nuclear weapons question in the Middle East, the Soviet Union is probably as uneasy about the impact of a non-proliferation treaty as is Israel. If both the Egyptians and the Israelis sign the agreement, the Soviets will be much relieved; if Israel signs after extracting something akin to a bilateral defense pact from the United States or if the United States becomes the major arms supplier to Israel, the Soviet Union will probably be forced to increase its conventional military aid to the Egyptians; if Israel refuses to sign a non-proliferation agreement under any conditions, the Soviet Union will be in a most difficult position. In the latter case, the Russians would be under great pressure to give the United Arab Republic a formal guarantee of nuclear protection. In other words, a non-proliferation treaty will introduce a new challenge to ever precarious political-military balance in the Middle East—and the result may be an increase in tension.

The countries discussed above were chosen primarily as a means of illustrating a method of looking at potential nuclear aspirants—a method which emphasizes the incentives and disincentives to build such weapons stemming from various combinations of national circumstances. A number of conclusions emerge from this approach which may be helpful when we turn to the possibilities and limitations for United States action in coping with the problem of the spread of nuclear weapons.

The first of these conclusions is one of definition. Webster's Dictionary defines "proliferate" as ". . . to grow by the rapid production of new parts, or new cells. . . ." The process of proliferation is thus organic and cumulative and the spread often in clusters. A look at the national circumstances of five of the leading contenders for nuclear status, however, indicates that the term proliferation is probably misleading in describing the process of nuclear spread. Unless a non-nuclear country considers itself directly threatened by an emerging nuclear power, it seems unlikely that the decision of one country to enter the nuclear weapons field will have much effect on another, even if that country is a neighbor.

National attitudes toward the acquisition of nuclear weapons are the end product of a highly complicated and often shifting array of national circumstances. To describe the process of nuclear spread as something infectious or organic is highly misleading. We are not dealing with a modern-day black plague slowly spreading its way across the earth's surface. If the desire for nuclear weapons is a disease then it is a disease where the causes are highly variable and the cure never the same. It would be well to put aside the term "proliferation" if it leads us to believe that there are common causes and therefore anything as simple as common cures for nuclear aspirations.

Second, estimates and predictions which attempt to block out the probable pace and pattern of nuclear spread over a number of years are of little use. A continuing assessment of the comparative nuclear capabilities of avowed or potentially hostile regional enemies as well as constant re-appraisals of national circumstances are necessary if we are to make any sense of the nuclear weapons problem. There are enough variables in national conditions to make long-range predictions of this or that country hazardous at best.

Third, if the country approach offered above is valid, then it is interesting to note that the incentive profiles of the countries discussed are essentially negative when it comes to a rough balance sheet between incentives and disincentives to acquiring nuclear weapons. And this list contains some of the foremost public candidates for nuclear status, such as West Germany and India. What this suggests is that if we take into account the total national circumstances of a country rather than dwelling on the technological barriers to weapons programs and extrapolating from the experiences of the present nuclear powers, what emerges most often is a very formidable gauntlet of barriers to any national decision to obtain nuclear weapons. This is not to say that the spread of nuclear weapons is not a significant problem, for some of the most compelling of national disincentives to acquiring nuclear weapons are highly unstable. But an imposing array of disincentives is invariably there and subject to bolstering through the actions of the major nuclear powers.

Finally, the major nuclear powers, despite their demonstrated inability to agree on international deterrents to nuclear spread, still retain the power to shape conditions which could inhibit the dispersion of nuclear weapons. Alliance arrangements, for example, where the alliance leader is a nuclear power can represent a significant barrier to the spread of nuclear weapons, if only because of the non-nuclear inertia such arrangements encourage. The major power, acting unilaterally or through formal or informal, bi- or multi-lateral arrangements, may have the power to make a significant difference in the decision of a non-nuclear nation on nuclear weapons. The critical ingredient in such actions is that they should be tailored to the problem—that is, that there are no common causes for the nuclear weapons "disease"—so the cures should be individual or at best regional.

The search for international cures, however, has thus far been the hallmark of American policy.

IV

The Legacy and the Challenge

In February of 1963, McGeorge Bundy, who as principal adviser to two presidents on international security affairs witnessed much of the North Atlantic Alliance's turmoil over the control of nuclear weapons, began a speech on Atlantic problems by saying: "An astonishing number of the great issues of international affairs turn on the way men see and value nuclear weapons." The point is relevant to an understanding of the course of American nuclear policy since the end of World War II.

According to the United States Arms Control and Disarmament Agency: "It has been the policy of every American national administration since the end of World War II to prevent the spread of nuclear weapons."[1] This conclusion, I'm afraid, is poorly rooted in the actual course of American policy over the past two decades. To describe how the United States has "seen" and "valued" nuclear weapons has been the objective of this study. In my own view, the evidence is conclusive that the United States' present policy of total resistance to the spread of nuclear weapons—a policy which has now taken on both the strength and the weakness of a religious crusade—is in fact of very recent origin.

The United States entered the nuclear era slightly awed with the magnitude of its own accomplishments and convinced that the feat of duplicating the Manhattan Project was beyond the skills and resources of most countries. We believed that even the major industrial countries, such as the Soviet Union, France, and Great Britain would be hard pressed to match our success, particularly if we carefully guarded our nuclear "secrets." The McMahon Act was the symbol of the United States' determination to preserve its nuclear monopoly as long as possible even though this legislation prevented cooperation even with the British, who had helped us develop the atomic bomb.

Whatever its faults, however, United States policy with regard to the spread of nuclear weapons was, at least until 1958, both consistent and understandable. It was a policy of confidence that a combination of the "atoms for peace" approach to the control of fissionable materials and the technological barriers to an independent nuclear weapons program would prevent what Mr. Dulles termed in 1957 the "promiscuous" spread of nuclear weapons. So assured, the United States could proceed to devising the nuclear defense of the Western Alliance in any way it saw fit—emplacement of missiles abroad, atomic warheads for NATO forces, the training of NATO forces in the use of atomic weapons. In short, a policy of maximum flexibility in the use of our nuclear weapons.

Consistent with this policy, the several minor modifications of the McMahon Act, first in 1954 and again in 1955, provided for an exchange of information concerning atomic weapons such as was required for the development of defense plans and the training of personnel of regional defense organizations. While some of our NATO Allies may have resented this policy of sharing only enough information with them to ensure their effective participation in the nuclear defense of the West, no one nation could complain too loudly that it was being discriminated against. All this was to change in 1958 when the United States began to turn to a policy of atomic discrimination among its Allies. Although Mr. Dulles was almost certainly not thinking of all our NATO Allies save Britain when he spoke in 1957 of the dangers of "promiscuous" proliferation, this, in fact, came to be the meaning of the term. Such discrimination could hardly have been well received by the non-Anglo-Saxon world.

In a number of ways, the Kennedy administration followed the basic outline of President Eisenhower's nuclear weapons policy. President Kennedy, like his predecessor, was fundamentally Atlantic "oriented." Kennedy also followed Eisenhower's post-1958 policy of holding Britain to be the only other legitimate member of the West's nuclear "elect"; but while Eisenhower apparently came to this position grudgingly, Kennedy embraced the idea of Britain's special status with enthusiasm. At the same time, however, Kennedy sought to pacify other Europeans by offering them a more formal role in the nuclear management of the Alliance. Unfortunately, the Kennedy administration destroyed whatever chance the nuclear sharing idea might have had in Europe with the Nassau agreement with Britain. In the process, the vigorous sales campaign also made "nuclear sharing" a dirty word on Capitol Hill.

One of President Johnson's most sensible decisions in the early months of his administration was to back away from the nuclear sharing project, and later to move the idea into a diplomatic limbo. President Johnson then turned from Kennedy's regional preoccupation to approaching the nuclear proliferation issue on a worldwide scale. A non-proliferation agreement became the centerpiece of Johnson's nuclear policy. This policy he has consistently pursued with great vigor and determination and now he is on the threshold of success.

With agreement between the United States and the Soviet Union on a non-proliferation agreement such a real possibility, it seems almost academic to reopen the question of why the United States wants such a treaty. Nevertheless, a review of the major arguments the United States has used to justify the need for non-proliferation may help to determine whether the objective was worth the effort. For there is no doubt that there will be "costs" as well as advantages to the United States from signing the present non-proliferation treaty. These costs include a further restriction on the use of our nuclear weapons and technology in maintaining and hopefully strengthening our Alliance relationships, or conceivably in the forming of new Alliance ties. For example, the West Germans undoubtedly feel that the United States, in pressing for such an agreement and cajoling the Germans to follow suit, is seriously, and unnecessarily, limiting America's ability to influence the course of Europe's nuclear weapons future. How can the United States hope to guide the Europeans in the nuclear weapons field if the United States so stringently limits the use of its own nuclear work and technology? All these arguments, of course, flow from the same basic assumption—that the mere signing of a non-proliferation agreement alone will achieve little more than exposing the fact that the United States and the Soviet Union can be equally pious when obliging themselves to refrain from doing something they would not have done in any event. Raymond Aron expressed his impatience with the United States' "double standard" with regard to nuclear weapons when he wrote in 1964:

> The vast majority of Americans, from the President and members of Congress to the man in the street, are spontaneously, unequivocally, and with a clear conscience opposed to the spread of nuclear weapons; and they passionately oppose the proliferation of these diabolical instruments not out of self-interest alone, but for the sake of all mankind. . . . I am not in favor of the dissemination of atomic weapons as such; but I am struck by the fact that Americans, even those least given to hypocrisy, do not feel bothered by the interpretation to which their attitude lends itself in the eyes of everyone else. If they are worried *now* about polluting the atmosphere, the fact remains that such scruples did not inhibit them as long as they felt it necessary to enlarge their own arsenal. Why, then, should others be more considerate?[2]

Why indeed? Aron's suggestion of hypocrisy in the recent American crusade for non-proliferation is echoed from another quarter. This time the criticism and mistrust come not from those who consider evoking the sake of all mankind as reason for the American position denying to others that which we consider vital to our own security as pure hypocrisy, but from those, such as the Indians, who believe the United States and the Soviet Union are pushing a non-proliferation treaty as a substitute for genuine progress in the disarmament field. An Indian spokesman made this point very clearly to the UN in 1965 before the UN Disarmament Commission:

> We want not only the prevention of further proliferation but also the reversal of present proliferation. . . . It is no use telling countries, some of which may be even more advanced in nuclear technology than China, that they should enter into a treaty which would stipulate that they must not acquire or produce these weapons. Again, it is no use telling them that their security will be safeguarded by one or other of the existing nuclear Powers. Such an assurance has to be really dependable. Moreover, nations are not interested in having another Hiroshima on their soil before an assurance of this nature could come into effect. Unless the nuclear Powers and would-be nuclear Powers undertake from now on not to produce any nuclear weapons or weapons delivery vehicles and, in addition, agree to reduce their existing stockpile of nuclear weapons, there is no way of doing away with the proliferation that has already taken place or of preventing further proliferation.

Again, in 1965, in a statement to the Eighteen Nation Disarmament Conference, the Indian delegate spoke of the "unrealistic and irrational proposition that a non-proliferation treaty should impose obligations only on non-nuclear countries while the nuclear powers continue to hold on to privileged status or club membership by retaining and even increasing their deadly stockpiles. . . ."[3] Indian resistance to a non-proliferation treaty that failed to achieve some sort of balance between the obligations of nuclear and non-nuclear powers has raised serious questions as to whether the Indians will sign the treaty as presently drafted.

The response of the United States to these evidences of distrust of and resistance to a non-proliferation treaty has been to press even harder for the attainment of a non-proliferation agreement and to offer a comprehensive program of disarmament and arms control measures to follow the signing of a non-proliferation agreement. The non-proliferation campaign has stressed the risks of a local or regional nuclear war which could ultimately drag in the great nuclear powers, the hazards to international health of testing, and the unfortunate diversion of vital resources if underdeveloped countries are forced into a weapons program. The answer to these dangers is a non-proliferation treaty, as Secretary of Defense McNamara explained in an interview which appeared in a Japanese magazine in August of 1966. Mr. McNamara's response to a question concerning the priority the United States gives to the attainment of a non-proliferation treaty is important as a concise statement of why the United States wants a non-proliferation treaty and what it hopes will be the effects of such a treaty:

Secretary McNamara: I think that [a non-proliferation treaty] is extremely important. It is in the interest of every nation in the world. I don't know any nation that wouldn't benefit from it. We would, the Soviets would, the nations that don't possess nuclear weapons would. This is true for several reasons, the most important of which is that the danger of nuclear war increases—I'd say geometrically—with the increase in the number of nations possessing independent nuclear forces. Therefore, if, for example, Japan, or India, or nations of the Middle East or Scandinavia or other areas of the world were to acquire nuclear weapons, the danger of nuclear war would be much greater—not only because they themselves had acquired them, and that in itself increases danger, but also because there would be a snowballing effect. If Nation A acquires nuclear weapons, very likely her potential adversary, Nation B, must acquire them, and then Nation C is concerned because Nation B might possibly have aggressive intentions with respect to Nation C, and therefore Nation C acquires them. The result is there can be a very rapid and dramatic expansion in the number of nuclear powers.

The way to prevent that is through a non-proliferation agreement which would be accepted by all nations of the world. We're very anxious to see such an agreement developed and accepted. There are subordinate reasons, however, that are important but not as important as the decrease in the risk of nuclear war that would result from such an agreement.

It's obvious that if nations are to develop nuclear weapons because there is no non-proliferation agreement, many of them will move to test in the atmosphere and this will contaminate the atmosphere with fallout. This is undesirable in itself and endangers not only the nation conducting the test but other nations in the world as well, to which the fallout is carried by the winds.

Finally *the financial cost of the development* of the nuclear warhead and all of the launch vehicles which are necessarily associated with it is very great indeed and, for almost every nation of the world, represents an undesirable diversion of resources from economic growth, which is the foundation of political stability in most nations of the world.

So for these reasons as well we are opposed to proliferation.[4]

The problem in accepting the arguments advanced by Mr. McNamara is that when one moves from the general to the specific the logic is more difficult to sustain. As long as we remain at the Nation A and Nation B level of analysis, visions of a catalytic war between the major powers touched off by a quarrel between any number of nuclear principalities remains a very vivid nightmare. To contemplate a world abounding with irresponsible pigmy powers rattling nuclear arms is certainly enough to justify the terrifying idea of a "geometric" increase in the dangers of nuclear war as the number of independent nuclear forces increases. Again, if nuclear "proliferation" is thought of as some virulent disease moving over the face of the globe it is then not difficult to foresee a breakdown of the limited test ban and an unfortunate diversion of the world's resources into weapons programs.

Clearly, such an abstract and universal approach to the spread of nuclear weapons leads naturally to abstract and universal remedies. A non-proliferation agreement is just such a universal remedy. The question is whether the solution is tailored to the problem.

It has been the argument of this study that the term "proliferation" is a misleading one in that it implies that the process of nuclear spread is organic and cumulative. A close look at a number of countries, including some leading contenders for nuclear status, indicates that national attitudes toward the acquisition of nuclear weapons are the end product of a highly complex and often shifting array of national circumstances.

If interest in a nuclear weapons program is a disease that is essentially a regional malady, not an international plague, then the causes are highly variable and the cure never the same. To maintain the flexibility necessary to correct an arms imbalance in one region by providing nuclear weapons cooperation to one or more of the antagonists may be as stabilizing to the global system as denying all arms cooperation—nuclear and conventional—is in another. In the pursuit of an international cure to what is essentially a regional problem, we have given up some of our flexibility in the use of our nuclear power.

To suggest that the problem of the spread of nuclear weapons is best dealt with on the regional level is not to underestimate the consequences for the international system of a further spread of weapons. New centers of atomic power will demand reassessments of the power balance on the part of the established nuclear powers, and possible de facto power realignments. The emergence of France and Communist China as nuclear powers has already produced a community interest between the United States and the Soviet Union. In the first case the United States and the Soviet Union have almost certainly over-reacted to the possibility that West Germany will try and follow the French. But it is the United States who is paying the cost in disruption to the Atlantic Alliance in pressing for a non-proliferation treaty while the Soviets will only profit by placing one more restraint on West Germany. In the Far East the potential is there for cooperation between the Soviet Union and the United States in creating a condition of regional security that will permit the Indians and the Japanese to forego duplicating the Chinese program. If such cooperation becomes a reality in regional security situations and can be extended into the field of arms control, then, only then, will a non-proliferation agreement be more than a pious piece of paper. A non-proliferation treaty itself will do none of the things Mr. McNamara suggests it will, and the sooner the United States realizes this the sooner we can begin to justify the costs in Alliance relations and international flexibility in the use of our nuclear power that a non-proliferation agreement will bring in its wake. Unlike a partial test ban, there is no reason to believe that a non-proliferation treaty in itself will even buy the international system time to deal with the problem of atomic nuclear spread. What it will buy is an atmosphere of common purpose between the major powers who sign the agreement and *most* of the non-nuclear world. But this atmosphere will be a highly volatile one, quick to dissipate if the great powers are content to believe with Mr. McNamara that a non-proliferation agreement will "prevent . . . a very rapid and dramatic increase in the number of nuclear powers."

The future of any international efforts to control the spread of nuclear weapons rests largely with the willingness of the United States and the Soviet Union to move together to give effect to the intentions of a non-proliferation treaty. With the realization that the problem is at least manageable if the abstract horrors of "nuclear proliferation" are translated into hard questions of *who, when,* and *why,* then the opportunities will arise to influence the national decisions of the countries considering nuclear weapons. Effective influence on national decisions will require strict attention to questions of regional security and regional prestige. Each set of countries faced with national decisions about nuclear weapons—the U.A.R. and Israel as one example, Communist China, India, and Japan as another— contain a unique blend of national circumstances, so efforts to diminish the rewards of acquiring nuclear weapons or the dangers of *not* acquiring them will have to be tailored to regional circumstances.

But what of the immediate "costs" of a non-proliferation treaty— and how can they be offset or possibly turned into gains? As already mentioned, the most obvious cost to the United States will be in our security relationships to friendly states. And this is a cost the United States must bear alone, for the Soviet Union has no allies whose political-military position will be affected by the restrictions of a non-proliferation pact. Only Czechoslovakia could be considered a potential nuclear aspirant in technological terms; but more importantly, no member of the Soviet Union's network of friends or protectorates—with the exception of the U.A.R., and marginally India—has the variety of national circumstances that would provoke an interest in the control of nuclear weapons. The United States has the problems here, notably with France, West Germany, Israel, Japan, and India. Our friends appreciate that we have given up flexibility in the use of our nuclear weapons assets. Whatever the other inconsistencies in his nuclear policy, the Eisenhower Administration did resist formally embracing a policy of total denial to our friends of the technology and the control of nuclear weapons; the Kennedy and Johnson Administrations, however, came to the conclusion that placing technological and political barriers before the further spread of nuclear weapons was more important. While Eisenhower rebuffed the French in 1958, he refrained from institutionalizing such rebuffs, thereby holding open his options. His successors have instead put a seal on America's ability to aid the development of independent nuclear forces—collective or national. Deprived of the option of assisting in the development of national or regional nuclear forces, the United States, for example, will now have to be unstinting in its resolve to stay in Europe with tactical nuclear weapons until such time as the Soviet military threat to Europe disappears. If we will not provide our friends with the means to defend themselves, we must be prepared to defend them where they want to be defended—*in* Europe, or *in* Asia.

Given these particular "costs" of a treaty, what can now be done to bolster our alliance relationships and to reassure those whose security is jeopardized by entering into the self-denying ordinance of a non-proliferation pact?

First, the United States must begin to adjust to the fact that there have been, and will be in the future, situations where no combination of incentives and restraints will deflect some nations from developing national nuclear weapons programs. In the case of France, for example, protestations of Alliance guarantees followed by diplomatic and technological pressure did not convince the French that they should not develop a national deterrent. Moreover, sheer pique at the French "effrontery" coupled with our policy of nuclear discrimination when the facts of the situation did not justify such discrimination, unnecessarily antagonized one of our oldest Allies. The United States simply did not behave in a mature way in dealing with French aspirations to be a nuclear power. After we had exhausted our stock of alternatives, we should have adjusted our policies to fit the realities of the French situation rather than harassing the French to a point where our ability to influence the future of the French nuclear program is severely limited. Can it really be in our interest to deny landing and transit rights in the United States to French aircraft carrying nuclear material or components to the nuclear test facilities in Tahiti?

The challenge for United States policy will be to know when to shift from a program of diminishing the rewards to acquiring a national nuclear weapons program to cooperating with the fledgling nuclear power in hopes of reducing the chances of nuclear accident or war. But the judgment and national maturity demanded in such a policy will be necessary if the United States is to avoid repeating the debacle of our French nuclear policy.

An important element in any policy of accepting with grace and intelligence the decision of certain states to develop nuclear weapons is to appreciate that if these states must have nuclear weapons, they had better have safe weapons. Imagine the possible consequences if a French aircraft had the same accident over the Mediterranean as an American bomber had in January of 1966 when four hydrogen bombs fell on Spain and its seacoast. Would there have been a nuclear catastrophe? In the future, what about Israel or Indian aircraft if these countries should decide to develop nuclear weapons? Can the United States afford not to share its hard-won and incredibly expensive knowledge of how to prevent unintentional nuclear weapons explosions? Equally important, the United States should consider sharing its knowledge of how to safeguard nuclear weapons devices in order to prevent unauthorized use. For example, the United States has developed at great effort and cost a system of electronic locks to be put on nuclear weapons to prevent unauthorized firing—the so-called Permission Action Link system. Would it not be in our interest and in the interest of world safety and security to help prevent the accidental detonation or unauthorized use of nuclear weapons developed by other countries? This is not a matter of encouraging the spread of nuclear weapons but adjusting to the realities and security demands of the spread that does occur. In other words, it would seem a cardinal principle of good sense and prudence if the United States would use its nuclear weapons knowledge to influence the development of national nuclear programs once we are certain a country is determined to have its own system. We have had to give up the possibility of transferring nuclear weapons to other countries in the interest of developing a de facto Russian-American cooperation. We are therefore doubly beholden to use the assets which remain to us to help prevent nuclear accidents and unpremeditated nuclear war.

Often mentioned as an answer to the question of what assurances or inducements we could offer to non-nuclear states for signing a non-proliferation pact is the extension of a nuclear guarantee. In a speech reporting the first Chinese nuclear test in 1964 President Johnson held out the promise of such guarantees when he said that "the nations that do not seek national nuclear weapons can be sure that if they need our strong support against some threat of nuclear blackmail, then they will have it." The problem with such a statement is that it is both ambiguous and not truly credible.

When Secretary Rusk was asked by the Vice-Chairman of the Joint Committee on Atomic Energy, Chet Holifield, what was meant by "our strong support," Mr. Rusk revealed some of the hazards of allowing presidential rhetoric to get out ahead of policy:

> It is our hope, Mr. Chairman, that, by something equivalent to a consensus of the international community, a country which does not have nuclear weapons, and which finds itself under aggressive threat by a country which does have nuclear weapons and specifically threatened with the use of nuclear weapons, would have the entire international community, including the United States, register its support in whatever appropriate way would be necessary in the circumstances.[5]

Considering the fact that the last three members of the nuclear club—Britain, France, and Communist China—were all sheltered by alliance guarantees offered by the two major powers and yet decided to go ahead and develop independent nuclear weapons, what possible effect could a nuclear "guarantee" have on a threatened India or Israel? Obviously, as Mr. Rusk went on to point out to the Committee, "there are some extremely fundamental questions here about what kinds of guarantees, what kinds of assurances, could give a non-nuclear power the repose it would need in order to stay out of the nuclear field while one of its rivals or potential enemies is making nuclear weapons." Responding to a question as to how such guarantees could actually be credible to a country threatened or potentially threatened by a new nuclear power, Secretary Rusk replied: ". . . If all five of the existing nuclear powers were to undertake such an obligation, then that would create a reasonably manageable situation."

While discounting the possibility that at least for the foreseeable future the five existing powers could agree on guarantees, Rusk did hold out the possibility that the United States, Great Britain, and the Soviet Union could provide such guarantees.

In his realistic appraisal of the feasibility and usefulness of nuclear guarantees as a means of controlling the spread of nuclear weapons, the Secretary comes close to the heart of the matter. He comes close in the sense that cooperation between some of the nuclear powers in bolstering the security and confidence of non-nuclear powers is realistic, particularly if this cooperation were given the general framework of a United Nations resolution. Such a resolution would be best suited to the practicalities of East-West cooperation if it specified only that if a non-nuclear state is attacked with nuclear weapons or threatened with a nuclear attack, the Security Council may authorize its members to take whatever action they deem necessary to repulse that attack or to lift the threat of nuclear blackmail. Because the national circumstances of countries facing the nuclear weapons questions are so different, the major powers acting together would have to adjust their responses to the individual situations. If such promises of assistance are to be credible to the non-nuclear state, however, they must not call for more than the nuclear powers are prepared to do. To ask the Indians to believe that the United States will pledge itself in advance to use its nuclear weapons to protect India from attack would be to defy the realities of the nuclear age and undermine Indian confidence in other commitments we may make.

Will the Indians—or the Israelis, or the Arabs—find such a guarantee credible? The skeptics will protest that such a commitment through the United Nations is specific only in the threat it describes, and totally unspecific in the response it promises. This argument misses the point. The combination of delineating a specific threat and promising only to take such action as the guarantors, acting individually or in concert with other parties to the resolution, deem necessary will, in fact, be the strength of such guarantees and give them credibility. What the non-nuclear state will have will be a strong psychological and political hold over those who offer the guarantee. And such a hold will act as a restraint on those who would threaten a non-nuclear state with nuclear weapons. By sharply limiting the guarantee to a pledge of response to a *non-nuclear* country subjected to *nuclear* blackmail or a *nuclear* attack, the pressure would be on a *nuclear* belligerent to keep nuclear weapons out of a dispute with a non-nuclear state. Defined in these terms such guarantees may be accepted by such potentially nuclear countries as Israel, the U.A.R., and India. There can be no certainty that a particular country will find a general guarantee enough. National circumstances are too different—and too changeable—to justify predictions as to whether this or that country will be satisfied by a United Nations nuclear guarantee. (Israel, as has been pointed out, will probably want a bilateral defense agreement from the United States.) But the existence or promise of such a guarantee may make the difference when a country is weighing the pros and cons of signing a non-proliferation pact—or living up to its terms. And this is reason enough for offering it.

While a United Nations resolution on nuclear guarantees will open the way to a de facto coalition between the Soviet Union and the United States to support non-nuclear states, the United States will also have to act alone in bolstering the security of the non-nuclear states. This can be done in a number of the traditional ways such as mutual defense pacts, collective security arrangements, and conventional military assistance. Nevertheless, we must also be prepared to use our nuclear weapons assets within the limitations of the non-proliferation pact.

One way is to be prepared to assign our nuclear weapons to areas where, as a result of the non-proliferation pact, we have increased obligations to see to the security of non-nuclear signatories. The United States in positioning its own nuclear weapons forces in Europe and assigning our NATO allies a nuclear mission under the double-key system has already made the kind of gesture other non-nuclear states, in other areas, may request. Such requests will be very difficult to turn down once a non-proliferation pact is a reality; as will requests from Europeans—particularly Germans—to maintain or even strengthen our nuclear strike forces in Europe. Given what the United States has asked of non-nuclear states in the non-proliferation treaty, it is incumbent on Washington to be receptive to any such requests. When Washington asks for the acquiescence of potential nuclear powers in the preservation of the major power nuclear monopoly, the United States acquires important responsibilities for their defense. Positioning of our nuclear weapons in areas where a non-nuclear power feels exposed and vulnerable to pressure from a new nuclear state will be one important and positive way of showing these countries that we are concerned about their security. We must be prepared in the aftermath of a non-proliferation treaty to use this option.

Another possibility, which could lead to a strengthening of the security of non-nuclear signatories of the treaty, has not yet been fully investigated, either technologically or politically. This is the possibility that the United States would deploy an anti-ballistic missile system outside the United States for the protection of countries threatened by new nuclear powers. Testing the feasibility of such an active defense system deployed outside the United States is not the same issue as asking whether the deployment of ABM's as *national* defense systems would slow the pace of nuclear proliferation. This obviously related question will be discussed below. An ABM active defense system outside of the United States raises different questions, because this system could be designed to defend signatories of the non-proliferation pact from direct ballistic missile blackmail.

Although the United States Navy has only begun to study the feasibility of such a system—the so-called Seaborne Anti-Ballistic Missile Interceptor System (SABMIS)—success with this concept could provide the United States with an invaluable tool in the protection of non-nuclear states. The concept now under consideration envisions mobile ABM systems with the required radars and missiles mounted on surface ships. The SABMIS would use the missile technology of Nike-X missile components—the Spartan and the Sprint—but not necessarily the same missile designs because of the need for a more maneuverable missile to intercept an incoming missile in mid-trajectory (i.e., on the way out rather than during final entry). Given the problems of building and operating the massive and complicated phased array radars used in missile defense, it may be necessary to place at least the radars on land. In the Pacific there are numerous islands, most of them U.S. owned or controlled, such as Okinawa, Guam, and the Palau Islands, where such radars could be installed.

The technological feasibility of a seaborne ABM system cannot be argued here, although the United States Navy has thought enough of the concept to invest in soliciting proposals from a number of major aero-space companies. If this system does prove workable, however, the United States should consider building and deploying it. Not only would a seaborne ABM missile force be testimony to our good faith in promising to protect non-nuclear states threatened by nuclear weapons, but unlike the double-key nuclear weapons arrangements now employed in Europe, the non-nuclear countries would have a high degree of confidence that a seaborne ABM defense would actually be used in their defense. The difference is that a seaborne ABM system would be solely a means of shooting down an incoming missile, whether a so-called "demonstration shot" designed to intimidate a population or an actual attack. These anti-ballistic missiles would no more provoke a widening of the engagement than a conventional surface-to-air missile against aircraft. Conversely, the two-key systems now employed with tactical nuclear weapons to be used against troops, military targets, and the like carry the very high risk of moving into a full nuclear exchange. Europeans and Asians know this and tend to put tactical nuclear weapons into the same category as strategic weapons, meaning the United States would not use them unless an all-out war was necessary. A nuclear ABM would not carry the same credibility problem. In other words, Europeans and Asians could have confidence that the United States would be willing to fire an ABM from a seaborne force at another nuclear weapon because the defensive intent would be so clear. Consequently, the development of a seaborne missile defense coupled with a nuclear guarantee through a United Nations resolution could become a meaningful "guarantee" to non-nuclear states looking for an alternative to developing their own nuclear weapons.

Once a non-proliferation pact is a reality the nuclear powers will, one hopes, begin to seek areas of potential cooperation which could give effect to the intent of the treaty. One such area of potential cooperation is that of nuclear free zones, or in the Communist parlance, "zones of peace." Proposals for such zones have taken many forms: Walter Ulbricht's Baltic "sea of peace" in 1955; the atomic free zone in Central Europe first put forward by Poland's Foreign Minister Rapacki in 1957; an Asian nuclear free zone advanced by Nehru in 1958 and echoed thereafter by the Communist Chinese; the "Unden Plan" first championed by the Swedish Foreign Minister in 1961; the Kekkonen Plan in 1963; a Soviet proposal in 1963 for a nuclear free zone in the Mediterranean. More recently, the emphasis has been on nuclear free zones for Africa and Latin America. The most important statement of African willingness to form a nuclear free zone came in 1964 when the African Heads of State and Government pledged their readiness to accept through an international treaty under the auspices of the UN the denuclearization of Africa. This pledge was reconfirmed at the Addis Ababa summit meeting in May of 1965 where the delegates declared "their readiness for a denuclearized zone in Africa."[6]

In Latin America there have been sporadic efforts since 1962 to attain a nuclear free zone. In 1963, for example, the Presidents of Mexico, Ecuador, Chile, Brazil, and Bolivia issued a joint declaration urging the formation of a nuclear free zone in Latin America. In 1965 Mexico and Brazil took the lead in organizing meetings held in Mexico City to consider ways of organizing a nuclear free zone.

On February 14, 1967, the Latin American countries signed the Treaty for the Prohibition of Nuclear Weapons in Latin America. Although United Nations Secretary General U Thant hailed the treaty as a "landmark," the demands of individual national circumstances have thus far blocked ratification of the treaty by all of its signatories. Cuba refused to participate; Argentina and Brazil have reservations about giving up the nuclear weapons option; while the major powers, including the United States, have had reservations about signing the protocols to the treaty which call upon the five nuclear powers to respect the prohibitions of the treaty and apply them within the geographical zone specified in the treaty.[7] The reasons for these reservations ranged from the U.K. suspicions that the treaty gives Argentina some claim over the British-held Falkland Islands to the United States' concern over the implied inclusion of Puerto Rico and the Virgin Islands. Most of these problems will undoubtedly be cleared up in time, but the experience is certainly an indication that even at the regional level non-proliferation efforts will encounter stubborn problems of differing—and often conflicting—national circumstances.

In approaching the formation of such zones in the future and responding to the desires of the possible participants, the United States should hold in mind what I consider the cardinal principle in dealing with the non-proliferation issue: each area of the world has its own particular problems and there are few common solutions. One system of verification that is appropriate to, say, Central Europe, where East-West tensions and security interests are high, would be utterly inappropriate for Africa. In the case of Africa and Latin America the United States should move quickly and put aside as generally unnecessary the strict verification demands we would require for Central Europe or the Baltic. Time is the key element here. The same sense of urgency that moved the United States and the Soviet Union to agree on a nuclear free zone in Antarctica and outer space should be there in responding to nuclear free zones in Africa and Latin America. We obviously cannot take the lead in the formation of such an arrangement, but we can encourage the process by stressing that in certain circumstances—and the Antarctica and Outer Space Treaties are models here—agreement may be more important than the verification language or the inconvenience to the movement of our nuclear weapons. For example, the United States' present position on verification in nuclear free zones requires ". . . that provision should be made for adequate verification, which would include procedures for following up on alleged violations in order to give reasonable assurance of compliance both to states included in the zone and to *those outside the zone who have* undertaken *to respect it.* "[8] The demand that the United States must be satisfied with the verification procedures of an agreement to which it is not a party rather than allowing the UN to be the judge seems unreasonable. If we want to encourage the formation of nuclear free zones—and there is every reason to do so—we should be careful to tailor our requirements to the circumstances rather than holding to some ideal model.

There remain a number of critical questions related to the pace and pattern of the spread of nuclear weapons and the effects of a non-proliferation pact: Would a qualitative arms escalation such as the United States and the Soviet Union are considering with the decision to develop and deploy anti-ballistic missile systems slow the pace of nuclear proliferation? What role will the International Atomic Energy Agency play after a non-proliferation treaty? And, finally, what position should the United States take with regard to the future of nuclear explosives for peaceful purposes? The first question suggests the possibility of again widening the technological gap between the nuclear haves and have-nots as a means of discouraging other countries from entering the nuclear arms field. A prohibition of national nuclear explosive programs for non-nuclear states presents the dilemma of asking the non-nuclear states to forswear the development of technology which may hold the key to enormous natural resources because this same technology could bring a non-nuclear country to the threshold of a weapons capability.

At this writing the United States and the Soviet Union are moving in the direction of escalating the arms race through the development and deployment of national anti-ballistic missile systems—the Nike-X and a comparable Soviet system. The first step has already been taken by the United States with the recent decision to build and deploy a limited or "thin" ABM decision. The military and political complexities of the national debate over whether the defense of the United States requires that we deploy some variety of an ABM system will not be discussed here. The relevant question for the non-proliferation issue is far simpler to pose and answer: What effect will the deployment of an anti-ballistic missile system in any form by the major powers have on non-nuclear states considering a weapons program and also on fledgling nuclear powers?

During his 1966 testimony before the Senate Subcommittee on Department of Defense Appropriations, Secretary of Defense McNamara spoke of the relevance of a "light" or "thin" defense to what he called the "Nth country nuclear threat." He said that an effective U.S. defense against a token force of ICBM's, such as the

Chinese or some as yet unnamed but unfriendly Nth country might deploy, ". . . might not only be able to negate that threat but might possibly weaken the incentives to produce and deploy such weapons altogether."[9] Mr. McNamara termed this variety of defense a "light Damage Limiting posture" and told the Committee that ". . . something less than a Full Fallout Shelter Program may be appropriate in a light Damage Limiting posture designed against small unsophisticated attacks." The Secretary then offered the following tentative conclusions concerning the effectiveness of "light" defense against the nuclear threat an Nth country could mount by the mid-1970's:

> A light anti-ballistic missile system using exoatmospheric interceptors and terminal defenses at a small number of cities offers promise of a highly effective defense against small ballistic missile attacks of the sort the Chinese Communists might be capable of launching within the next decade. The initial investment and five year operating cost (including R & D) would be about $8–10½ billion, depending on the number of cities defended and the density of the area coverage.[10]

Mr. McNamara's argument must be read carefully in order to make the necessary distinction between an "effective defense" against an Nth country and the possibility of weakening incentives "to produce and deploy such weapons altogether." The first point is well taken as long as the threatening country has only an unsophisticated ballistic missile system, and for at least the next ten years this will include every country except Russia and the United States. As for the possibility of weakening incentives to produce nuclear weapons, however, this assumption is highly questionable even in the case where the potential or emerging nuclear power has as its most likely adversary either the United States or the Soviet Union. For example, it is highly questionable whether the deployment of ABM systems by the Soviet Union or the United States will act as a significant restraint on the plans of the French (who face the Soviet Union) or the Chinese (who face the United States and the Soviet Union).

In the past, obvious discrepancies in power and capability had no significant effect on the decisions of France and Communist China to enter the nuclear weapons field. The national circumstances of these two countries, particularly their alliance relationships, were such that a national weapons program was considered essential. The overall political-diplomatic context which so strongly favored a decision to build nuclear weapons was simply more powerful than one of its parts—the military equation. Since the basic circumstances which prompted the decision of the Chinese and the French have not changed, we can only assume that they will continue with their weapons program despite an ABM deployment by the United States or the Soviet Union.

As for countries whose nuclear strike force would not be directed against a major nuclear power, what the United States and the Soviet Union do about defending themselves with ABM's is quite irrelevant. India's incentives to build a nuclear weapon, for example, would hardly be weakened by a United States decision to defend the continental United States with ABM's. In fact, the opposite might be true. The construction by the United States and the Soviet Union of an anti-ballistic missile system limited to defending their national territory could be taken by the non-nuclear states as a return to the concept of a "fortress America" or a "fortress Russia." Isolated from a United States or a Soviet Union who have taken to defending themselves from each other, or from Communist China, with an ABM system, non-nuclear countries may be prompted to developing their own nuclear means of defense.

Therefore, the United States should approach the decision on ABM's fully aware of the possible effect on the non-proliferation issue. What has been argued here, assuming the development of an ABM system which proves effective against limited missile forces, is that an ABM system, perhaps a seaborne force, deployed outside the United States for the defense of non-nuclear countries against nuclear attack or blackmail could be of considerable help in persuading non-nuclear countries to stay that way; and conversely, an ABM deployment limited to a continental defense of the United States could have the opposite effect. However, at least the first half of this conclusion will have to remain tentative until the feasibility of a seaborne ABM force has been tested. As for ABM deployment within the United States—be it "light" or "heavy"—the case for such a step will have to be justified on other grounds than as a barrier to further spread of nuclear weapons.

Less dramatic than the ABM issue, but of considerable significance, will be the effects of the non-proliferation treaty on the institutional character of the International Atomic Energy Agency.

As mentioned, IAEA had its origins in President Eisenhower's 1953 Atoms for Peace speech. Eisenhower hoped that by controlling the sources of nuclear energy the world would be spared a proliferation of nuclear powers. IAEA was founded on this assumption and proceeded to organize along the lines of controlling the flow of nuclear materials while assisting research programs. As a result of the emphasis, the Agency's nuclear safeguards program, first set up in 1961, remained the stepchild of IAEA, and as late as 1967 had a team of only 13 inspectors inspecting facilities which produced only 6 percent of the world's plutonium output.

Beginning in 1963, however, the United States made a vigorous effort to increase the role of IAEA in the development of an international system of safeguards. This new emphasis on safeguards rather than controlling the raw materials was a major shift from the Eisenhower approach. Since coming to office, President Johnson has urged repeatedly that all countries accept for their nuclear facilities the application of the safeguard procedures of the International Atomic Energy Agency or an equivalent system. He has also urged that ". . . all transfers of nuclear materials or equipment for peaceful purposes to countries which do not have nuclear weapons be under IAEA or equivalent international safeguards. At the same time, the major nuclear powers should accept in increasing measure the same international safeguards they recommend for other states." As for the control of the production of fissionable materials for use in weapons, President Johnson has advocated a "verified halt" in the production of weapon-grade materials and the ". . . transfer of large quantities of fissionable material to peaceful purposes, under international safeguards." [11]

Although the effectiveness of present international inspection systems in the production of nuclear weapons material has been questioned, there is no doubt that as the large atomic power plants gradually come under the IAEA international cooperation confidence will be strengthened. For its part, the United States has recently put all of its non-military reactors under IAEA. The United States also has 32 bilateral agreements for safeguarding the nuclear cooperation we provide. It is significant that 27 of these bilateral agreements call for or contemplate the transfer of the inspection role to the IAEA. This policy of encouraging the development of an international system of inspection is actively supported by the U.S. Joint Committee on Atomic Energy. The Vice Chairman of that Committee, Chet Holifield, believes that if we support the IAEA ". . . a vigorous, experienced, and respected International Agency will evolve whose control system will be administered strictly and impartially and with a minimum of injury to national pride."[12] As the agent who will be responsible for assuming these increased and unexpected responsibilities, the International Atomic Energy Agency has neither fully developed its safeguards system nor the staff to police a non-proliferation pact. Time, a tenfold increase in the number of inspectors, and a comparable increase in budget (in the 1967 annual budget, the Agency's safeguards division received only $550,000 of the $12 million budget) will soon bring IAEA to a point where the Agency will be able to assume the role of assuring compliance with the non-proliferation treaty.

As for the future, it is clearly in the United States' interest to pursue an active policy of encouraging worldwide support of an international system of cooperation in the control of atomic materials as called for in our non-proliferation treaty. We have come a long way from the days of 1953 when President Eisenhower presented his "Atoms for Peace" plans to the General Assembly of the United Nations. Fortunately there are few American leaders today who believe that the "Atoms for Peace" approach is any substitute for constructive policies in other areas. Nevertheless, there are real dangers for international cooperation and acceptance of the non-proliferation treaty if the nuclear powers should be tempted to turn IAEA into *their* police force. The idea that IAEA's responsibilities under a non-proliferation treaty should be well defined has been given a Congressional boost by Senator Pastore, Chairman of the Joint Committee on Atomic Energy. Senator Pastore voiced his objections to the wording of an earlier U.S. draft which required that "each of the states party to this treaty undertakes to cooperate in facilitating the application of international safeguards." The Senator has called this language "vague and noncommittal," and called for the following new language:

> *Each of the non-nuclear states* party to the treaty undertakes to accept International Atomic Energy Agency or similar safeguards on *all* of their nuclear activities.[13]

The intent of Senator Pastore's proposal is clear: The safeguards clauses of the non-proliferation treaty should be directed primarily at guaranteeing that the non-nuclear powers stay non-nuclear. No one can dispute the worthy purpose here; but by limiting the obligations to the non-nuclear powers the proposal releases the nuclear powers from any responsibility for bringing their own facilities into the structure of international cooperation; and this waiver will reinforce the suspicion of many non-nuclear countries that the major powers are only interested in perpetuating their atomic oligopoly. It seems imperative, therefore, if a non-proliferation treaty is to work, that the major powers must specify their willingness to hasten the day when a majority of the world's atomic power plants will be under international supervision. The United States has taken an important step in this direction by offering to bring all of its large non-military reactors under IAEA safeguards. If this action is followed by a strongly worded inspection clause in the non-proliferation pact, the future of international safeguards will be bright indeed.

Finally, a few things remain to be said about the relevance of a comprehensive test ban to the pace and pattern of the spread of nuclear weapons, and about the more specific but closely and hotly debated issue of the future of the civilian uses of nuclear explosives—known as the Plowshare Program in the United States.

On the question of a comprehensive or total nuclear ban, President Johnson has said emphatically that the United States "persists in its belief that the perils of proliferation would be materially reduced by an extension of the limited test ban treaty to cover undergound nuclear tests. For such an extension, the United States will require only the number and kind of inspections which modern science shows to be necessary to assure that the treaty is being faithfully observed." [14] Yet in spite of remarkable advances in seismology, including the development of a seismic "array" system that if deployed widely would be able to distinguish with a high degree of reliability between natural seismic shocks and man-made nuclear explosions, the United States Government remains badly divided on whether a comprehensive test ban would be in our national interest.

At one point in 1966, for example, the United States was seriously considering offering a treaty banning nuclear underground explosions above a certain blast force—approximately 20 kilotons or greater. The champions of this proposal argued that this variation of the so-called "threshold" idea would be acceptable to the United States without inspections (which the Soviets have steadfastly refused to consider) because these larger blasts were sure to be detected and identified by the new generation of seismic stations.[15] This proposal was apparently the victim of divided council within the U.S. government and has been quietly shelved.[16] Furthermore, the evidence is strong that even if the United States were convinced of the absolute reliability of detecting and identifying underground nuclear tests above a certain threshold—in the 20 or even 50 kiloton range—domestic political and military objections would prevent the signing of such an agreement.

The problem with U.S. acceptance of a comprehensive test ban in any form stems from the circumstances surrounding the Senate's approval of the Limited Test Ban in 1963. In the administration's efforts to convince the Congress that U.S. security would not be jeopardized by the partial test ban, administration officials and scientists repeatedly made or agreed with statements that unrestricted underground testing was vital to our national security. As a result of these hearings the so-called treaty safeguards program was established under the watchful eye of the Joint Committee on Atomic Energy. In the Committee's 1966 report on these safeguards, Senator Jackson referred to one of the safeguards as ". . . the conduct of comprehensive, aggressive, and continuing underground test programs." This underground program has included over 100 tests. In stressing the importance of continuing underground testing, including some between 200 kilotons and 1 megaton, Senator Jackson, speaking for the Joint Committee, pointed out that without underground testing two of the other "safeguards"—the maintenance of modern weapons laboratories and the maintenance of facilities to resume atmospheric testing—"would have little chance of being successfully implemented." The report's final comments on an underground testing program are important if we are to judge sensibly the prospects and implications of a comprehensive test ban for the pace of nuclear spread:

A nuclear weapons program, like all scientific endeavors, is a living and growing effort. Weapons research cannot be stockpiled or kept on a shelf against a future rainy day. Progress in science and technology cannot go far without experiments.

In this connection, and in the light of continued underground testing by the Soviet Union and atmospheric testing by France and Communist China, a warning is necessary: The Senate must take a long hard look at any proposals for total test ban treaties to be fully informed at an early stage of all the ramifications of particular proposals, and to see that we do not consent to any arrangements or provisions which operate against our vital national security interests.[17]

Clearly, the Joint Committee on Atomic Energy was not talking about the problems of verification, but about the potential threat to American security of a comprehensive test ban under any circumstances. There is little doubt that under present, or even immediately foreseeable circumstances, a total test ban would be rejected by the U.S. Senate even if the dissenting Senators were convinced that such a treaty would be, in the President's words, "faithfully observed."

The controversy over the future of peaceful uses of nuclear explosives is closely tied to the issue of a comprehensive test ban—or, more precisely, to the technological barrier thesis, basic to the rationale of the comprehensive test ban approach. While a good case can be made for a comprehensive test ban as an all but insurmountable barrier to a national weapons program, the suppression of the technology of nuclear explosive devices for commercial purposes is unwise if we want an effective non-proliferation pact.

First of all, the United States appreciates, on the basis of its own Plowshare Program, that nuclear explosives programs hold the possibility of developing enormous natural resources. At the present time, conventional methods of converting shale oil deposits to useful petroleum products are prohibitively expensive. If the use of nuclear explosives to extract oil from oil shale proves feasible, the United States Bureau of Mines estimates that about two trillion barrels of oil will be available from the shale deposits in three western states. At our present rate of use of 11 million barrels per day, this new oil supply would be enough for at least 500 years.[18] Using nuclear explosives, the United States may also be able to more than double U.S. recoverable gas reserves, provide needed storage for billions of cubic feet of gas, and mine additional millions of tons of copper.[19] More widely known is the use of nuclear explosives to build harbors, canals, and clear mountain passes. It is important to point out here that both the experiments with recovering national resources and the process itself, should it prove feasible, involve fully contained nuclear explosions which would not, by any definition, violate the partial test ban. On the other hand, the excavation portion of the Plowshare Program would require an amendment to the test ban treaty.

The future of the Plowshare program thus presents the United States with a dilemma which was well expressed by Mr. Adrian Fisher, Deputy Director of the U.S. Arms Control and Disarmament Agency, in a speech given before the Eighteen Nation Disarmament Conference on the relationship of nuclear explosive devices to a non-proliferation treaty. Mr. Fisher said that it was an "inescapable technological fact" that "the development of nuclear explosives for any purpose by a state which does not now possess nuclear weapons would inevitably involve the acquisition by that state of a nuclear weapons capability."[20] The answer to this problem as far as the United States is concerned would be for the established nuclear powers to develop the nuclear explosives and then offer to make available the service to non-nuclear states at a price well below development costs.

> The United States believes that, if and when peaceful applications of nuclear explosives that are permissible under test ban treaty limitations prove technically and economically feasible, nuclear weapons states should make available to other states nuclear explosive services for peaceful applications. Such a service would consist of performing the desired nuclear detonation under appropriate international observation, with the nuclear device remaining under the custody and control of the state which performs the service.[21]

In order to prevent what the American delegation at Geneva has called "the proliferation of contrivances useful as nuclear weapons,"[22] the United States and the Soviet Union have been unyielding in their resistance to any provision in a non-proliferation pact that would permit the non-nuclear signatories to develop and test nuclear explosive devices. This position has aroused not only the ire of many of the non-nuclear states, who feel strongly that a national nuclear explosive program is vital to the development of their commercial nuclear program, but also the displeasure of the U.S. Joint Committee on Atomic Energy. In its report to the Congress authorizing appropriations for the AEC Fiscal Year 1968, the Joint Committee, after recommending an increase of $8.5 million in operating funds for Plowshare, complained:

> The committee feels compelled to point out this year, as it did last, its deep concern that planned Plowshare excavation experiments have not been conducted. Two experiments planned in this connection were not carried out in Fiscal Year 1966. Again, in fiscal 1967—despite the expenditure of nearly $6 million for excavation experiments—no cratering experiments were executed. Approximately $2,000,000 has been totally wasted in getting ready for the Cabriolet cratering event. A hole for this event was dug, the device was emplaced, and on February 10, 1967, the event was postponed ". . . in order"—in the words of the executive branch—"to avoid any possibility of complicating the current discussions concerning a non-proliferation treaty. . . ."

The Committee then went on to recommend:

> If the funds provided are not to be expended for experiments, but instead are to be consumed in delays, then the committee believes that the Administration should cancel the excavation portion of the Plowshare program. Of course, one logical result of any such action would be the necessary withdrawal of the President's offer to share this technology with the world. The Committee would very much regret such negative action being taken, but it cannot stand idly by while the taxpayers' money is being wasted.[23]

Considering the widespread resistance to the Administration's attitude on nuclear explosives, it is incumbent on the United States to reconsider its position. In any such reconsideration a number of factors are important. First, the United States should recall that the Anglo-American Draft Treaty on the Discontinuance of Nuclear Weapons Tests of April 18, 1961, and a similar proposal offered on August 27, 1962 (which was the working draft at Moscow in 1963), allowed for explosions of nuclear devices for peaceful purposes under certain conditions of safeguards. The 1961 draft, for example, provided for an elaborate system of reporting and observing of the sites as well as inspection of the device itself by each of the original parties to the proposed treaty—the Soviet Union, the United Kingdom, and the

United States. The similarities between the provisions of this draft and the Treaty for the Prohibition of Nuclear Weapons in Latin America are striking; yet in 1961 the United States suggested the concept, in 1965 opposed it. Moreover, the United States was to change its position on peaceful nuclear devices during the 1963 partial test ban negotiations. The switch was made without consultation with interested parties not in Moscow, and only at the demand of the Soviet Union. In return, the United States sought and won approval of a proposal easing the amending process—and this modification was asked for, according to observers, in order to facilitate a restoration at some future date of the authority to develop nuclear explosives. Clearly the record of how we arrived at our present steadfast position on nuclear explosives is damaging to our case as to why this prohibition is necessary.

Second, in considering the problem of nuclear explosive devices the United States is clinging to the discredited technological barrier thesis. There is no disputing the contention of United States officials at Geneva that "the technology of making nuclear explosive devices is essentially indistinguishable from the technology of making nuclear weapons." But this connection between devices and weapons would only be important if weapons technology could only be acquired by testing nuclear devices. If there is anything the United States should know after more than twenty years of dealing with nuclear technology, it is that technology is there for the asking—or reading—if a country wants weapons badly enough. It is simply impossible to suppress technology for very long. Better the United States deal with the highly particular circumstances which motivate a country to want nuclear weapons rather than vainly trying to deny them the technology.

If this analysis is correct, the United States should seriously consider modifying its position on the nuclear explosive devices, perhaps by going back to the provisions of the 1961 Anglo-American draft treaty which permitted the civilian use of nuclear devices under strict safeguards. In order to preserve the integrity of the partial test ban, this modification could be limited to fully contained nuclear explosives such as those designed for oil and gas recovery. In time, as the technology of "clean" explosives improves, the modification could be extended to excavation projects.

Would the Russians refuse such modifications? Perhaps. But

we should remember that the Russians have already reversed themselves on Plowshare, and now feel that nuclear explosives can be used for peaceful purposes. Considering the Soviet Union's recent enthusiasm for IAEA inspections and safeguards, the Russians would be hard pressed to object to a provision of the non-proliferation pact which allowed for the detonation of nuclear devices for peaceful purposes closely supervised by IAEA.

Although the United States cannot keep the technology of nuclear weapons from countries that want it, a comprehensive test ban may be the one realistic hope of those who would slow the pace of nuclear proliferation by the creation of technical barriers.

A comprehensive test ban, unlike a prohibition on the testing of nuclear explosives for peaceful purposes, goes to the heart of nuclear weapons issues. For the non-nuclear states a comprehensive test ban *will not* deprive them of weapons technology, but it *will* block the opportunity to test and to develop nuclear weapons with confidence in the reliability of the weapons product. The word "reliability" is used here because a comprehensive test ban could not prevent a country from building a nuclear weapon. However, a country would probably withdraw from a comprehensive test ban treaty before building a nuclear weapon it could not test.

In considering a comprehensive test ban, the qualification of a *worldwide* acceptance of a total test ban is important. It also assumes, and this is a reasonable assumption, that progress in seismology will reach a point of achieving President Johnson's condition that we have assurance that the treaty is "being faithfully observed." Indeed, the technological skill of detection and identification will probably be with us long before there is international acceptance of the principle of a total test ban. And such an across-the-board acceptance of a comprehensive test ban including *all* the nuclear powers is essential if a total test ban is to serve—not wound—the cause of international peace and stability. To move from a partial test ban signed by most to a comprehensive test ban signed by all will take years of effort in correcting disparities in power to a point where all nations will feel confident enough, or technologically frustrated enough, to sign such a treaty.

Raymond Aron has called America's preoccupation with the spread of nuclear weapons an "obsession." "Over-reaction" is probably a more accurate, if less vivid, description of the United States' behavior when it finally realized that nuclear secrets had been reduced to nuclear cookbooks. Tormented by thoughts of a world filled with pigmy states rattling nuclear arms, the United States abandoned a policy of flexible use of its nuclear weapons assets and sought a universal remedy to prevent the further spread of nuclear weapons. A non-proliferation treaty became the centerpiece of U.S. nuclear policy. And to get such a treaty we are prepared to accept restrictions on the use of our nuclear resources, while simultaneously giving security guarantees to those non-nuclear states who would sign a non-proliferation pact. In spite of new restrictions and new responsibilities, however, a non-proliferation pact can mark the beginning of a new era of international cooperation and security if we grasp what we achieve—and will *not* achieve—in such an agreement.

What we will purchase with a non-proliferation treaty is an atmosphere of concern, and an opportunity to work with the Soviet Union in turning a very pious and unwieldy treaty into a de facto coalition—a coalition that will best serve its interests if we keep firmly in mind the highly individual national circumstances surrounding a country's interest in nuclear weapons. Could we and the Russians create this atmosphere of mutual concern without a formal, international treaty so unsuited in conception to the complexities of nuclear proliferation? Probably not. In this period of hesitant cooperation, both the United States and the Soviet Union prefer international agreements to bilaterals. A non-proliferation pact will give an ideologically comfortable framework for East-West cooperation. The content of the treaty will not be as important as the fact that it has the support of most members of the United Nations.

As for the future, until the day comes when all the nations are prepared to sign a comprehensive test ban and begin to scale down their nuclear armaments we must abandon thoughts of returning to the more congenial world of great power monopoly over nuclear weapons. Instead, we must be prepared to tolerate the acquisition of nuclear weapons in one place, resist it in another, perhaps even tacitly encourage it in a third. We must also be prepared to amend the non-proliferation treaty to meet the legitimate requests of other countries.

The nuclear proliferation issue is manageable if we reduce the abstract horror of it to the specifics of policy choices. Living in an age where our nuclear monopoly is being slowly eroded is a test of national maturity. We have no recourse but to meet this test.

Notes

Introduction

1. *New York Times,* March 23, 1963.
2. United States Senate, *The Nuclear Test Ban Treaty,* Hearing before the Committee on Foreign Relations United States Senate, GPO: Washington, D.C., 1963, p. 47. Emphasis mine.
3. *New York Times,* October 7, 1964.
4. William C. Davidson, Marvin I. Kalkstein, Christoph Hohenemser, *The Nth Country Problem and Arms Control,* Washington, D.C., 1958; and Leonard Beaton and John Maddox, *The Spread of Nuclear Weapons,* Chatto and Windus, London, 1962.
5. R. N. Rosecrance (ed.), *The Dispersion of Nuclear Weapons,* Columbia University Press, New York, 1964.

Chapter I

1. Ambassade de France, Service de Presse et d'Information. Speeches and Press Conferences, No. 210, November 3, 1964, p. 3.
2. For a discussion of the moral dilemma for the United States, see John C. Bennett (ed.), *Nuclear Weapons and the Conflict of Conscience,* New York, Scribner, 1962; and William J. Nagle, *Morality and Modern Warfare: The State of the Question,* Baltimore, Helicon Press, 1960.
3. See James Brown Scott (ed.), *Proceedings of the Hague Peace Conferences: The Conference of 1899,* Oxford University Press, 1920, passim.
4. See J. H. Rothschild, *Tomorrow's Weapons,* McGraw-Hill (New York, 1961) passim, esp. pp. xi–xv, and 21–27.
5. *Proceedings of the Hague Peace Conferences: The Conference of 1899,* pp. 283, 296.
6. See U.S. Department of State, *A Report on the International Control of Atomic Energy* (The Acheson-Lilienthal Report), Publication 2498, Washington, 1946.
7. Randolph S. Churchill (ed.), *Europe Unite, Speeches in 1947 and*

1948 by Winston S. Churchill, Boston, Houghton Mifflin Co., 1950, pp. 414–415.

8.   United States Atomic Energy Commission, *In the Matter of J. Robert Oppenheimer*, Transcript of the Hearing before the Personnel Security Board, April 12, 1954, through May 6, 1954. Testimony of K. T. Compton, pp. 257–258.

9.   For figures of United States expenditures in the atomic energy field, see United States Atomic Energy Commission, *Annual Report to Congress— 1963*, GPO, Washington, 1964, p. 470.

10.   This tendency to downgrade was painfully evident as Washington recorded the shock of learning that the first Chinese device contained Uranium 235, rather than only the more simply acquired plutonium, raising the possibility that the Chinese have a gaseous-diffusion plant—a feat thought beyond them at this stage.

11.   See *Soviet Atomic Espionage*, U.S. Government Printing Office, Washington, 1951; Gordon Dean, *Report on the Atom*, Knopf, New York, 1953; Alan Moorehead, *The Traitors*, London, 1952, as examples.

12.   From a speech delivered by Dr. Seaborg at the Palais des Nations, Geneva, Switzerland, September 8, 1964, AEC Press Release, No. S–20–64, dated September 14, 1964, p. 2.

13.   *Ibid.*, p. 3.

14.   *Ibid.*, pp. 5–6.

15.   See Arnold Kramish, "The Emergent Genie," in *The Dispersion of Nuclear Weapons*, edited by R. N. Rosecrance, Columbia University Press, New York, 1964, for a distinguished account of the changing technology of nuclear weapons development.

16.   Kramish, "The Emergent Genie," p. 264.

17.   Letter can be found in the verbatim record of the Conference of the Eighteen Nation Committee on Disarmament, ENDC/PV, 268, p. 41.; the Pastore resolution is S. Res. 179, 89th Cong., 2nd Sess.

18.   General Assembly Resolution 715 (VIII), November, 1953.

19.   *Documents on Disarmament, 1945–1959*, 2 vols. Department of State, Washington, D.C., 1960, vol. 1, p. 650.

20.   *Ibid.*, p. 410.

21.   *The New York Times*, February 24, 1955, p. 14.

22.   *Documents on Disarmament*, vol. 1, pp. 700, 702.

23.   *Dulles Papers*, Category IX, Conference Dossiers, 1957—June, 1958. Remarks of the Secretary of State at the opening session of the Western European Chiefs of Mission meeting in Paris, May 9, 1958.

24.   From the text of a letter from Dwight D. Eisenhower to Senator

Henry M. Jackson and Congresswoman Edna Kelly, dated May 17, 1966. *Congressional Record*, October 4, 1966, p. 24084.

25. For text see the *United States Statutes at Large*, 85th Congress, 2nd Session, 1958, Vol. 72, Part I, Public Laws and Reorganization Plan, pp. 276–279, GPO, Washington, 1959; for a brief legislative history see *United States Code: Congressional and Administrative News*, 85th Congress, Second Session, 1958, Vol. II, pp. 2816–2850.

26. *United States Code*, P. 2818.

27. *Amending the Atomic Energy Act of 1954*, Hearing before the Subcommittee on Agreements for Cooperation of the Joint Committee on Atomic Energy, 85th Congress, 2nd Session, Government Printing Office, Washington, 1958, p. 5.

28. *United States Statutes at Large*, 85th Congress, 2nd Session, 1958, p. 276. Emphasis mine.

29. *The United States Code*, 85th Congress, 2nd Session, 1958, p. 2826.

30. *Ibid.*, p. 2827.

31. *Amending the Atomic Energy Act of 1954*, p. 183. Senator John O. Pastore put it a bit more delicately: ". . . I will tell you very frankly I do not know how you can strike up this bilateral with the United Kingdom without making this broad amendment that we are talking about, [and] that all of us do so with our tongues in our cheek. We realized that. But we cannot pick out a nation and write it into law. If we could do that and get away with it, we would do it. . . ." Pp. 186–187.

32. On France, see *Amending the Atomic Energy Act of 1954*, pp. 342–343, 353. About the only explanation offered as to what the United States would say if France developed its own nuclear device and then came to the United States for aid similar to that provided the British was that in such an eventuality France would probably not be able to provide the "necessary security guarantees." P. 343.

33. *Amending the Atomic Energy Act of 1954*.

34. *Amending the Atomic Energy Act of 1954*, p. 464.

35. *Ibid.*, pp. 453–454. Emphasis mine.

36. *Ibid.*, pp. 342–343.

37. *United States Code*, 85th Congress, 2nd Session, 1958, Vol. 11, p. 2827.

38. For Britain and the inspection problem see *The New York Times*, February 14, 1965.

39. *Dulles Papers*, Category IX, Conference Dossiers, Special Subjects, dated June 30, 1958.

40. Premier Georges Pompidou before the National Assembly, April

20, 1966. Ambassade de France Service de Presse et d'Information. Speeches and Press Conferences Nos. 243A and 245A, April 1966, pp. 18–19.

41.   Department of State Bulletin, Vol. XXXVII, No. 954 of October 7, 1957, p. 556.

42.   Official Records of the General Assembly, Sixteenth Session, Annexes, agenda item 81, p. 3.

43.   Official Records of the General Assembly, Thirteenth Session, First Committee, 945th to 972nd meetings; and *Ibid.*, Plenary Meetings, 779th meeting. The Irish resolution may be found as Document A/C.1/L. 206 of October 17, 1958.

44.   UN Document A/C.1/L. 206.

45.   UN Document A/C.1/L. 207 to draft resolution A/C.1/L. 205.

46.   Verbatim Record of the 970th meeting of the First Committee. A/C.1/PV. 970 of October 31, 1958, p. 76.

47.   A/C.1/PV. 969, p. 27.

48.   *Ibid.*

49.   UN Document A/3974, pp. 8, 11.

50.   *Dulles Papers*, Category IX, Conference Dossiers, 1957–June, 1958. From a paper prepared for the Secretary by Gerald Smith, Counselor of the Policy Planning Staff of the Department of State, entitled "Outline of the World Situation." This paper was prepared for the Secretary's use before an Executive Session of the Senate Foreign Relations Committee, January of 1958. Paper dated January 3, 1958, pp. 12, 14.

51.   *Ibid.*, p. 15. These were the Thor and Jupiter missiles.

52.   Official Records of the General Assembly, Fourteenth Session, First Committee, 1054th to 1056th meeting.

53.   *Ibid.*, Plenary Meeting, 841st meeting, 1959. The Irish resolution may be found as A/C.1/L. 235/ Rev. 3. A/C.1/L. 235/ Rev. 3.

54.   Official Records of the General Assembly, Fourteenth Session, First Committee, 1054th to 1056th meetings. Verbatim record of the First Committee, A/C.1/PV. 1056, p. 36.

55.   Official Records of the General Assembly, Fifteenth Session, Annexes, agenda item 73, p. 27.

56.   Verbatim Record of the 1135th meeting of the First Committee, A/C.1/PV. 1135, pp. 37–38.

Chapter II

1.   John F. Kennedy in a review of Liddell Hart's *Deterrent or Defense* in the *Saturday Review*, September 3, 1960, p. 17.

2.   Address by President Kennedy to the Canadian Parliament, Ottawa,

of May 17, 1961, in *Nuclear Weapons*, ed. A. E. M. Duynstee, Western European Union Assembly, Committee on Defense Questions and Armaments, November, 1964, p. 49.

3. *Nuclear Weapons*, p. 61. From a speech Mr. Bundy, who was at the time President Kennedy's Special Assistant for National Security Affairs, made to the General Assembly of the North Atlantic Treaty Organization on September 27, 1962.

4. "Nominations of Robert R. Bowie and U. Alexis Johnson," August 16, 23, 1966, Committee on Foreign Relations, Washington, 1966, p. 9.

5. Arthur M. Schlesinger, Jr., *A Thousand Days: John F. Kennedy in the White House*, Houghton Mifflin Company, 1965, p. 904.

6. Schlesinger, p. 905.

7. Theodore C. Sorensen, *Kennedy*, Harper and Row, 1965, p. 734.

8. For the arguments of the State Department's Legal Adviser that no change in the status of the East German regime occurred as a result of the Test Ban Treaty, see U.S. Congress, *Hearing: Nuclear Test Ban Treaty*, 88th Congress, 1st Session, GPO 1963, pp. 15–17, 968–976.

9. Harold K. Jacobson and Eric Stein, *Diplomats, Scientists, and Politicians: The United States and the Nuclear Test Ban Negotiations*, University of Michigan Press, Ann Arbor, 1966, p. 457.

10. Letter dated August 8, 1963, in *Nuclear Test Ban Treaty*, Hearing before the Committee on Foreign Relations, United States Senate, p. 3.

11. *Ibid.*, p. 19.

12. *Ibid.*, p. 108.

13. *Nuclear Test Ban Treaty*, p. 118.

14. *AEC Authorizing Legislation for Fiscal Year 1965*, Hearing before the Joint Committee on Atomic Energy, Congress of the United States, Part I, GPO, Washington, 1964, pp. 121–125.

15. *Nuclear Test Ban Treaty*, p. 580.

Chapter III

1. National Planning Association, *1970 Without Arms Control*, Planning Pamphlet No. 104, Washington, D.C., 1958; *The Nth Country Problem and Arms Control*, Planning Pamphlet No. 108, Washington, 1960.

2. *The Nth Country Problem and Arms Control*, p. 26.

3. *Ibid.*, p. 23.

4. Beaton and Maddox, p. 65.

5. *Ibid.*, pp. 98–181. Israel was also included.

6. R. N. Rosecrance, *The Dispersion of Nuclear Weapons*, p. 3.

7.   *Indian and Foreign Review*, II, No. 16 of June 1, 1965, p. 5.

8.   *Overseas Hindustan Times*, January 7, 1965.

9.   *Nucleonics*, XXII, No. 10 (October, 1964), 60–61.

10.   *Ibid.*, no. 4 (April, 1964), 27; *India News*, February 6, 1965; *Christian Science Monitor*, August 5, 1965; *Hindustan Times*, March 26, 1963; *Atomic News Digest*, New Delhi (November, 1962).

11.   *India News*, January 30, 1965.

12.   See the *New York Times* of November 8, 1964, the *Christian Science Monitor* of November 9 and 27, 1964, for reports of the debate within India. Senator Robert F. Kennedy has cited India as one of the two nations (Israel was the other) that ". . . already possess weapons-grade fissionable material, and could fabricate an atomic device within a few months." *Congressional Record*, 89th Congress, 1st Session, June 23, 1965.

13.   *Indian Foreign Policy*, Selected Speeches of Jawaharlal Nehru, September 1946–April 1961, Government of India, Publications Division, Ministry of Information and Broadcasting, 1961. From a speech during debate on foreign affairs in Lok Sabha, September 30, 1954.

14.   *Nucleonics*, XXII (October, 1964), 60–61.

15.   See the remarks of Asoka Mehta, Deputy Chairman of India's Planning Commission, *Indian and Foreign Review*, II, no. 14. of May 1, 1965.

16.   P. C. Chakravarti, *India's China Policy*, Bloomington, Indiana University Press, 1962, pp. vii–viii.

17.   Myron Weiner, "Whither India? Unity and Diversity," *Asia*, No. 3. (Spring, 1965), 2.

18.   Quoted in Weiner Levi, "Indian Neutralism Reconsidered," *Pacific Affairs*, XXXVIII, no. 2 (Summer, 1964), 142.

19.   ENDC/PV. 298, p. 13, May 23, 1967.

20.   *India News*, May 12, 1967.

21.   *Nucleonics*, XX, No. 8 (August, 1962), 40–41; *Ibid.*, XXIII, No. 4 (April 1965), 27.

22.   See in particular the excerpts from a Japanese mother's account of the death in 1954 of her 13-year-old daughter who was exposed to nuclear radiation at Hiroshima in 1945. *Contemporary Japan*, XXVII, no. 2 (March, 1962), 298–299. This is just one example of such accounts which are given wide distribution in the Japanese press. Although estimates vary, approximately 150,000 Japanese have died as the result of the Hiroshima and Nagasaki bombings. For an excellent account of Japan and the atom see Douglas H. Mendel, *The Japanese People and Foreign Policy*, Berkeley, University of California Press, 1961, Chapter VI, pp. 151–168.

23.   In 1954 after the fishing boat incident 70% of the Japanese polled by the newspaper *Asahi* believed that the Japanese people may be injured by atomic testing. Three years later, 87% of those interviewed felt that every kind of nuclear test should be prohibited. Allan B. Cole, *Japanese Opinion Polls with Socio-Political Significance, 1947–1957*, vol. 1, pp. 703, 763.

24.   *Japan Report*, VIII, No. 5, March 25, 1962.

25.   Quoted in Mendel, 93.

26.   For an excellent discussion of these changes in Japanese attitudes see Masao Maruyama, *Thought and Behaviour in Modern Japanese Politics*, London, Oxford University Press, 1963; and I. I. Morris, *Nationalism and the Right Wing in Japan*, London, Oxford University Press, 1960, passim.

27.   I. I. Morris, 263.

28.   See Kei Wakaizumi, "The Problem for Japan," in *A World of Nuclear Powers?* ed. Alastair Buchan, American Assembly, Columbia University, Prentice-Hall Inc. 1966, pp. 77–78.

29.   *Japan Times Weekly*, April 1, 1967. See also *Ibid.*, February 18, 1967.

30.   Speech before the Japanese Diet, March 14, 1967.

31.   See the *Washington Post*, March 10 and 15, 1967; *Japan Times Weekly*, February 2, 1967; *London Times*, March 15, 1967.

32.   *The Politics of Western Defense*, New York, Praeger, 1962, pp. 79–80. Italics added.

33.   Theo Sommer, "The Objectives of Germany," in *A World of Nuclear Powers?* pp. 39–54.

34.   *The Israel Digest*, IV, No. 1 (January 6, 1961). See also the *New York Times* of December 22, 1960, and the *Jewish Observer and Middle East Review* of December 23, 1960, pp. 3–4.

35.   *New York Times*, May 14, 1966. In 1963 Shimon Peres, Israeli Deputy Minister of Defense, pointed with pride to the fact that the Ministry of Defense was heavily engaged in "propulsion, electronics, and ballistics" programs and ". . . shared in the national effort directed at the expansion and dispersal of industry, improving technical standards, and increasing production."

36.   See Shimon Peres, "Problems of Israel's Security," *Israel Year Book—1963*, pp. 212–213.

37.   Peres, 212.

38.   Quote in the *Jewish Observer and Middle East Review*, December 23, 1960, pp. 3–4.

Chapter IV

1. "To Prevent the Spread of Nuclear Weapons", United States Arms Control and Disarmament Agency, Publication 26, September 1965 p. iii.

2. Raymond Aron, *The Great Debate: Theories of Nuclear Strategy*, Doubleday, New York, 1965, p. 237.

3. See, for example, the Swedish Statement before the UN Disarmament Commission on May 20, 1965, and *Washington Post*, February 18, 1965, for the remarks of Japanese Deputy Foreign Minister Takezo Shimoda.

4. Quoted in the Department of State Bulletin, of August 29, 1966, pp. 304–305.

5. *Non-proliferation of Nuclear Weapons*, Joint Committee on Atomic Energy, p. 12.

6. ENDC/180 of August 22, 1966.

7. Text and additional protocols may be found in *The United Nations and Disarmament*, United Nations, Office of Public Information, New York, 1967, pp. 309–322.

8. From a statement made by William C. Foster, Director of the Arms Control and Disarmament Agency, in Committee I (Political and Security) of the UN General Assembly on December 1, 1965. Quoted in *Department of State Bulletin*, January 17, 1966, p. 104.

9. Statement of Secretary of Defense Robert S. McNamara before the Senate Subcommittee on Department of Defense Appropriations on the Fiscal Year 1967–71 Defense Program and 1967 Defense Budget, p. 56.

10. *Ibid.*, p. 58.

11. From President Johnson's message to the Eighteen Nation Disarmament Committee, January 27, 1966. ENDC/165 of January 27, 1966, pp. 2–3. See also ENDC/172 of March 8, 1966, for particulars of U.S. proposal on the transfer of fissionable materials to peaceful uses.

12. *Congressional Record*, August 2, 1966, pp. 17078–82.

13. *Ibid.*, March 9, 1967.

14. From President Johnson's message to the Eighteen Nation Disarmament Committee, January 27, 1966.

15. See an article by John W. Finney, *New York Times*, June 14, 1966, for the best account of this proposal.

16. *New York Times*, June 30, 1966.

17. *Congressional Record*, October 18, 1966, vol. 112, no. 179, pp. 26318–26321. Quotation on 26319.

18. J. H. East, Jr., and E. D. Gardner, *Oil Shale Mining, Rifle, Colorado, 1945–56*, U.S. Department of the Interior, Bureau of Mines, Bulletin

611, 1964, as cited in R. E. Smith "Three Possible Engineering Applications of Nuclear Explosives in the Shale Oil Industry," Sandia Corporation, SC–RR–65–657, October 1966, p. 5.

19. See Paul A. Witherspoon "Economics of Nuclear Explosives in Developing Underground Gas Storage," Laurence Radiation Laboratory, University of California at Livermore, UCRL–14877, July 29, 1966.

20. 280th ENDC Plenary Meeting on August 9, 1966.

21. *Ibid.*

22. ENDC/PV. 295, March 21, 1967, p. 92.

23. Report by the Joint Committee on Atomic Energy, 90th Congress, 1st Session, Report No. 349, June 23, 1967, pp. 45–46.

Appendix I:

United States of America
Draft Treaty on the Non-Proliferation of Nuclear Weapons,
January 18, 1968.

The States concluding this Treaty, hereinafter referred to as the "Parties to the Treaty,"

Considering the devastation that would be visited upon all mankind by a nuclear war and the consequent need to make every effort to avert the danger of such a war and to take measures to safeguard the security of peoples,

Believing that the proliferation of nuclear weapons would seriously enhance the danger of nuclear war,

In conformity with resolutions of the United Nations General Assembly calling for the conclusion of an agreement on the prevention of wider dissemination of nuclear weapons,

Undertaking to co-operate in facilitating the application of International Atomic Energy Agency safeguards on peaceful nuclear activities,

Expressing their support for research, development and other efforts to further the application, within the framework of the International Atomic Energy Agency safeguards system, of the principle of safeguarding effectively the flow of source and special fissionable materials by use of instruments and other techniques at certain strategic points,

Affirming the principle that the benefits of peaceful applications of nuclear technology, including any technological by-products which may be derived by nuclear-weapon States from the development of nuclear explosive devices, should be available for peaceful purposes to all Parties to the Treaty, whether nuclear-weapon or non-nuclear-weapon States,

Convinced that in furtherance of this principle, all Parties to this Treaty are entitled to participate in the fullest possible exchange of scientific information for, and to contribute alone or in co-operation with other States to, the further development of the applications of atomic energy for peaceful purposes,

Declaring their intention that potential benefits from any peaceful applications of nuclear explosions should be available through appropriate international procedures to non-nuclear-weapon States Party to this Treaty on a non-discriminatory basis and that the charge to such Parties for the explosive devices used should be as low as possible and exclude any charge for research and development,

Declaring their intention to achieve at the earliest possible date the cessation of the nuclear arms race,

Urging the cooperation of all States in the attainment of this objective,

Desiring to further the easing of international tension and the strengthening of trust between States in order to facilitate the cessation of the manufacture of nuclear weapons, the liquidation of all their existing stockpiles, and the elimination from national arsenals of nuclear weapons and the means of their delivery pursuant to a Treaty on general and complete disarmament under strict and effective international control,

Have agreed as follows:

ARTICLE I

Each nuclear-weapon State Party to this Treaty undertakes not to transfer to any recipient whatsoever nuclear weapons or other nuclear explosive devices or control over such weapons or explosive devices directly, or indirectly; and not in any way to assist, encourage, or induce any non-nuclear-weapon State to manufacture or otherwise acquire nuclear weapons or other nuclear explosive devices, or control over such weapons or explosive devices.

ARTICLE II

Each non-nuclear-weapon State Party to this Treaty undertakes not to receive the transfer from any transferor whatsoever of nuclear weapons or other nuclear explosive devices or of control over such weapons or explosive devices directly, or indirectly; not to manufacture or otherwise acquire nuclear weapons or other nuclear explosive devices; and not to seek or receive any assistance in the manufacture of nuclear weapons or other nuclear explosive devices.

ARTICLE III

1. Each non-nuclear-weapon State Party to the Treaty undertakes to accept safeguards, as set forth in an agreement to be negotiated and concluded with the International Atomic Energy Agency in accordance with the Statute of the International Atomic Energy Agency

and the Agency's safeguards system, for the exclusive purpose of verification of the fulfillment of its obligations assumed under this Treaty with a view to preventing diversion of nuclear energy from peaceful uses to nuclear weapons or other nuclear explosive devices. Procedures for the safeguards required by this Article shall be followed with respect to source or special fissionable material whether it is being produced, processed or used in any principal nuclear facility or is outside any such facility. The safeguards required by this Article shall be applied on all source or special fissionable material in all peaceful nuclear activities within the territory of such State, under its jurisdiction, or carried out under its control anywhere.

2.   Each State Party to the Treaty undertakes not to provide: (a) source or special fissionable material, or (b) equipment or material especially designed or prepared for the processing, use or production of special fissionable material, to any non-nuclear-weapon State for peaceful purposes, unless the source or special fissionable material shall be subject to the safeguards required by this Article.

3.   The safeguards required by this Article shall be implemented in a manner designed to comply with Article IV of this Treaty, and to avoid hampering the economic or technological development of the Parties or international cooperation in the field of peaceful nuclear activities, including the international exchange of nuclear material and equipment for the processing, use or production of nuclear material for peaceful purposes in accordance with the provisions of this Article and the principle of safeguarding set forth in the Preamble.

4.   Non-nuclear-weapon States Party to the Treaty shall conclude agreements with the International Atomic Energy Agency to meet the requirements of this Article either individually or together with other States in accordance with the Statute of the International Atomic Energy Agency. Negotiation of such agreements shall commence within 180 days from the original entry into force of this Treaty. For States depositing their instruments of ratification after the 180-day period, negotiation of such agreements shall commence not later than the date of such deposit. Such agreements shall enter into force not later than eighteen months after the date of initiation of negotiations.

ARTICLE IV

1.   Nothing in this Treaty shall be interpreted as affecting the inalienable right of all the Parties to the Treaty to develop research, production and use of nuclear energy for peaceful purposes without discrimination and in conformity with Articles I and II of this Treaty.

2.   All the Parties to the Treaty have the right to participate in the fullest possible exchange of scientific and technological information for the peaceful uses of nuclear energy. Parties to the Treaty in a position to do so shall also cooperate in contributing alone or together with other States or international organizations to the further development of the applications of nuclear energy for peaceful purposes, especially in the territories of non-nuclear-weapon States Party to the Treaty.

ARTICLE V

Each Party to this Treaty undertakes to cooperate to insure that potential benefits from any peaceful applications of nuclear explosions will be made available through appropriate international procedures to non-nuclear-weapon States Party to this Treaty on a non-discriminatory basis and that the charge to such Parties for the explosive devices used will be as low as possible and exclude any charge for research and development. It is understood that non-nuclear-weapon States Party to this Treaty so desiring may, pursuant to a special agreement or agreements, obtain any such benefits on a bilateral basis or through an appropriate international body with adequate representation of non-nuclear-weapon States.

ARTICLE VI

Each of the Parties to this Treaty undertakes to pursue negotiations in good faith on effective measures regarding cessation of the nuclear arms race and disarmament, and on a treaty on general and complete disarmament under strict and effective international control.

ARTICLE VII

Nothing in this Treaty affects the right of any group of States to conclude regional treaties in order to assure the total absence of nuclear weapons in their respective territories.

ARTICLE VIII

1.   Any Party to this Treaty may propose amendments to this Treaty. The text of any proposed amendment shall be submitted to the Depositary Governments which shall circulate it to all Parties to

the Treaty. Thereupon, if requested to do so by one-third or more of the Parties to the Treaty, the Depositary Governments shall convene a conference, to which they shall invite all the Parties to the Treaty, to consider such an amendment.

2. Any amendment to this Treaty must be approved by a majority of the votes of all the Parties to the Treaty, including the votes of all nuclear-weapon States Party to this Treaty and all other Parties which, on the date the amendment is circulated, are members of the Board of Governors of the International Atomic Energy Agency. The amendment shall enter into force for each Party that deposits its instrument of ratification of the amendment upon the deposit of instruments of ratification by a majority of all the Parties, including the instruments of ratification of all nuclear-weapon States Party to this Treaty and all other Parties which, on the date the amendment is circulated, are members of the Board of Governors of the International Atomic Energy Agency. Thereafter, it shall enter into force for any other Party upon the deposit of its instrument of ratification of the amendment.

3. Five years after the entry into force of this Treaty, a conference of Parties to the Treaty shall be held in Geneva, Switzerland, in order to review the operation of this Treaty with a view to assuring that the purposes and provisions of the Treaty are being realized.

ARTICLE IX

1. This Treaty shall be open to all States for signature. Any State which does not sign the Treaty before its entry into force in accordance with paragraph 3 of this Article may accede to it at any time.

2. This Treaty shall be subject to ratification by signatory States. Instruments of ratification and instruments of accession shall be deposited with the Governments of _____, which are hereby designated the Depositary Governments.

3. This Treaty shall enter into force after its ratification by all nuclear-weapon States signatory to this Treaty, and 40 other States signatory to this Treaty and the deposit of their instruments of ratification. For the purposes of this Treaty, a nuclear-weapon State is one which has manufactured and exploded a nuclear weapon or other nuclear explosive device prior to January 1, 1967.

4. For States whose instruments of ratification or accession are deposited subsequent to the entry into force of this Treaty, it shall

enter into force on the date of the deposit of their instruments of ratification or accession.

5. The Depositary Governments shall promptly inform all signatory and acceding States of the date of each signature, the date of deposit of each instrument of ratification or of accession, the date of the entry into force of this Treaty, and the date of receipt of any requests for convening a conference or other notices.

6. This Treaty shall be registered by the Depositary Governments pursuant to Article 102 of the Charter of the United Nations.

ARTICLE X

1. Each Party shall in exercising its national sovereignty have the right to withdraw from the Treaty if it decides that extraordinary events, related to the subject matter of this Treaty, have jeopardized the supreme interests of its country. It shall give notice of such withdrawal to all other Parties to the Treaty and to the United Nations Security Council three months in advance. Such notice shall include a statement of the extraordinary events it regards as having jeopardized its supreme interests.

2. Twenty-five years after the entry into force of the Treaty, a Conference shall be convened to decide whether the Treaty shall continue in force indefinitely, or shall be extended for an additional fixed period or periods. This decision shall be taken by a majority of the Parties to the Treaty.

ARTICLE XI

This Treaty, the English, Russian, French, Spanish and Chinese texts of which are equally authentic, shall be deposited in the archives of the Depositary Governments. Duly certified copies of this Treaty shall be transmitted by the Depositary Governments to the Governments of the signatory and acceding States.

In witness whereof the undersigned, duly authorized, have signed this Treaty.

Done in _____ at _____ this _____ of
_____.

Appendix II

Treaty for the Prohibition of Nuclear Weapons in Latin America

Preamble

In the name of their peoples and faithfully interpreting their desires and aspirations, the Governments of the States which have signed the Treaty for the Prohibition of Nuclear Weapons in Latin America,

Desiring to contribute, so far as lies in their power, towards ending the armaments race, especially in the field of nuclear weapons, and towards strengthening a world at peace, based on the sovereign equality of States, mutual respect and good neighbourliness,

Recalling that the United Nations General Assembly, in its resolution 808 (IX), adopted unanimously as one of the three points of a co-ordinated programme of disarmament "the total prohibition of the use and manufacture of nuclear weapons and weapons of mass destruction of every type,"

Recalling that militarily denuclearized zones are not an end in themselves but rather a means for achieving general and complete disarmament at a later stage,

Recalling United Nations General Assembly resolution 1911 (XVIII), which established that the measures that should be agreed upon for the denuclearization of Latin America should be taken "in the light of the principles of the Charter of the United Nations and of regional agreements,"

Recalling United Nations General Assembly resolution 2028 (XX), which established the principle of an acceptable balance of mutual responsibilities and duties for the nuclear and non-nuclear powers, and

Recalling that the Charter of the Organization of American States proclaims that it is an essential purpose of the organization to strengthen the peace and security of the hemisphere,

---

Signed at Mexico City on 14 February 1967.

Convinced:

That the incalculable destructive power of nuclear weapons has made it imperative that the legal prohibition of war should be strictly observed in practice if the survival of civilization and of mankind itself is to be assured,

That nuclear weapons, whose terrible effects are suffered, indiscriminately and inexorably, by military forces and civilian population alike, constitute, through the persistence of the radioactivity they release, an attack on the integrity of the human species and ultimately may even render the whole earth uninhabitable,

That general and complete disarmament under effective international control is a vital matter which all the peoples of the world equally demand,

That the proliferation of nuclear weapons, which seems inevitable unless States, in the exercise of their sovereign rights, impose restrictions on themselves in order to prevent it, would make any agreement on disarmament enormously difficult and would increase the danger of the outbreak of a nuclear conflagration,

That the establishment of militarily denuclearized zones is closely linked with the maintenance of peace and security in the respective regions,

That the military denuclearization of vast geographical zones, adopted by the sovereign decision of the States comprised therein, will exercise a beneficial influence on other regions where similar conditions exist,

That the privileged situation of the signatory States, whose territories are wholly free from nuclear weapons, imposes upon them the inescapable duty of preserving that situation both in their own interests and for the good of mankind,

That the existence of nuclear weapons in any country of Latin America would make it a target for possible nuclear attacks and would inevitably set off, throughout the region, a ruinous race in nuclear weapons which would involve the unjustifiable diversion, for warlike purposes, of the resources required for economic and social development,

That the foregoing reasons, together with the traditional peace-loving outlook of Latin America, give rise to an inescapable necessity that nuclear energy should be used in that region exclusively for peaceful purposes, and that the Latin American countries should use their right to the greatest and most equitable possible access to this new source of energy in order to expedite the economic and social development of their peoples,

Convinced finally:

That the military denuclearization of Latin America—being understood to mean the undertaking entered into internationally in this Treaty to keep their territories forever free from nuclear weapons—will constitute a measure which will spare their peoples from the squandering of their limited resources on nuclear armaments and will protect them against possible nuclear attacks on their territories, and will also constitute a significant contribution towards preventing the proliferation of nuclear weapons and a powerful factor for general and complete disarmament, and

That Latin America, faithful to its tradition of universality, must not only endeavour to banish from its homelands the scourge of a nuclear war, but must also strive to promote the well-being and advancement of its peoples, at the same time co-operating in the fulfilment of the ideals of mankind, that is to say, in the consolidation of a permanent peace based on equal rights, economic fairness and social justice for all, in accordance with the principles and purposes set forth in the Charter of the United Nations and in the Charter of the Organization of American States,

Have agreed as follows:

Obligations

ARTICLE 1

1. The Contracting Parties hereby undertake to use exclusively for peaceful purposes the nuclear material and facilities which are under their jurisdiction, and to prohibit and prevent in their respective territories:

(a) The testing, use, manufacture, production or acquisition by any means whatsoever of any nuclear weapons, by the Parties themselves, directly or indirectly, on behalf of anyone else or in any other way; and

(b) The receipt, storage, installation, deployment and any form of possession of any nuclear weapon, directly or indirectly, by the Parties themselves, by anyone on their behalf or in any other way.

2. The Contracting Parties also undertake to refrain from engag-

ing in, encouraging or authorizing, directly or indirectly, or in any way participating in the testing, use, manufacture, production, possession or control of any nuclear weapon.

Definition of the Contracting Parties

ARTICLE 2

For the purposes of this Treaty, the Contracting Parties are those for whom the Treaty is in force.

Definition of territory

ARTICLE 3

For the purposes of this Treaty, the term "territory" shall include the territorial sea, air space and any other space over which the State exercises sovereignty in accordance with its own legislation.

Zone of application

ARTICLE 4

1. The zone of application of the Treaty is the whole of the territories for which the Treaty is in force.

2. Upon fulfilment of the requirements of article 28, paragraph 1, the zone of application of the Treaty shall also be that which is situated in the western hemisphere within the following limits (except the continental part of the territory of the United States of America and its territorial waters): starting at a point located at 35° north latitude, 75° west longitude; from this point directly southward to a point at 30° north latitude, 75° west longitude; from there, directly eastward to a point at 30° north latitude, 50° west longitude; from there along a loxodromic line to a point at 5° north latitude, 20° west longitude; from there directly southward to a point at 60° south latitude, 20° west longitude; from there directly westward to a point at 60° south latitude, 115° west longitude; from there directly northward to a point at 0° latitude, 115° west longitude; from there along a loxodromic line to a point at 35° north latitude, 150° west longitude; from there directly eastward to a point at 35° north latitude, 75° west longitude.

Definition of nuclear weapons

ARTICLE 5

For the purposes of this Treaty, a nuclear weapon is any device which is capable of releasing nuclear energy in an uncontrolled manner and which has a group of characteristics that are appropriate for use for warlike purposes. An instrument that may be used for the transport or propulsion of the device is not included in this definition if it is separable from the device and not an indivisible part thereof.

Meeting of signatories

ARTICLE 6

At the request of any of the signatories, or if the Agency established by article 7 should so decide, a meeting of all the signatories may be convoked to consider in common questions which may affect the very essence of this instrument, including possible amendments to it. In either case, the meeting will be convoked by the General Secretary.

Organization

ARTICLE 7

1. In order to ensure compliance with the obligations of this Treaty, the Contracting Parties hereby establish an international organization to be known as the "Agency for the Prohibition of Nuclear Weapons in Latin America," hereinafter referred to as "the Agency." Only the Contracting Parties shall be affected by its decisions.

2. The Agency shall be responsible for the holding of periodic or extraordinary consultations among member States on matters relating to the purposes, measures and procedures set forth in this Treaty and to supervision of compliance with the obligations arising therefrom.

3. The Contracting Parties agree to extend to the Agency full and prompt co-operation in accordance with the provisions of this Treaty, of any agreements they may conclude with the Agency and of any agreements the Agency may conclude with any other international organization or body.

4. The headquarters of the Agency shall be in Mexico City.

Organs

ARTICLE 8

1. There are hereby established as principal organs of the Agency a General Conference, a Council and a Secretariat.

2. Such subsidiary organs as are considered necessary by the General Conference may be established within the purview of this Treaty.

The General Conference

ARTICLE 9

1. The General Conference, the supreme organ of the Agency, shall be composed of all the Contracting Parties; it shall hold regular sessions every two years, and may also hold special sessions whenever this Treaty so provides, or, in the opinion of the Council, the circumstances so require.

2. The General Conference:

(a) May consider and decide on matters or questions covered by the Treaty, within the limits thereof, including those referring to powers and functions of any organ provided for in this Treaty.

(b) Shall establish procedures for the control system to ensure observance of this Treaty in accordance with its provisions.

(c) Shall elect the members of the Council and the General Secretary.

(d) May remove the General Secretary from office if the proper functioning of the Agency so requires.

(e) Shall receive and consider the biennial and special reports submitted by the Council and the General Secretary.

(f) Shall initiate and consider studies designed to facilitate the optimum fulfilment of the aims of this Treaty, without prejudice to the power of the General Secretary independently to carry out similar studies for submission to and consideration by the Conference.

(g) Shall be the organ competent to authorize the conclusion of agreements with Governments and other international organizations and bodies.

3. The General Conference shall adopt the Agency's budget and fix the scale of financial contributions to be paid by member States, taking into account the systems and criteria used for the same purpose by the United Nations.

4.   The General Conference shall elect its officers for each session and may establish such subsidiary organs as it deems necessary for the performance of its functions.

5.   Each member of the Agency shall have one vote. The decisions of the General Conference shall be taken by a two-thirds majority of the members present and voting in the case of matters relating to the control system and measures referred to in article 20, the admission of new members, the election or removal of the General Secretary, adoption of the budget and matters related thereto. Decisions on other matters, as well as procedural questions, and also determination of which questions must be decided by a two-thirds majority, shall be taken by a simple majority of the members present and voting.

6.   The General Conference shall adopt its own rules of procedure.

The Council

ARTICLE 10

1.   The Council shall be composed of five members of the Agency elected by the General Conference from among the Contracting Parties, due account being taken of equitable geographical distribution.

2.   The members of the Council shall be elected for a term of four years. However, in the first election three will be elected for two years. Outgoing members may not be re-elected for the following period unless the limited number of States for which the Treaty is in force so requires.

3.   Each member of the Council shall have one representative.

4.   The Council shall be so organized as to be able to function continuously.

5.   In addition to the functions conferred upon it by this Treaty and to those which may be assigned to it by the General Conference, the Council shall, through the General Secretary, ensure the proper operation of the control system in accordance with the provisions of this Treaty and with the decisions adopted by the General Conference.

6.   The Council shall submit an annual report on its work to the General Conference as well as such special reports as it deems necessary or which the General Conference requests of it.

7.   The Council shall elect its officers for each session.

8.   The decisions of the Council shall be taken by a simple majority of its members present and voting.

9.   The Council shall adopt its own rules of procedure.

The Secretariat

ARTICLE 11

1. The Secretariat shall consist of a General Secretary, who shall be the chief administrative officer of the Agency, and of such staff as the Agency may require. The term of office of the General Secretary shall be four years and he may be re-elected for a single additional term. The General Secretary may not be a national of the country in which the Agency has its headquarters. In case the office of General Secretary becomes vacant, a new election shall be held to fill the office for the remainder of the term.

2. The staff of the Secretariat shall be appointed by the General Secretary, in accordance with rules laid down by the General Conference.

3. In addition to the functions conferred upon him by this Treaty and to those which may be assigned to him by the General Conference, the General Secretary shall ensure, as provided by article 10, paragraph 5, the proper operation of the control system established by this Treaty, in accordance with the provisions of the Treaty and the decisions taken by the General Conference.

4. The General Secretary shall act in that capacity in all meetings of the General Conference and of the Council and shall make an annual report to both bodies on the work of the Agency and any special reports requested by the General Conference or the Council or which the General Secretary may deem desirable.

5. The General Secretary shall establish the procedures for distributing to all Contracting Parties information received by the Agency from governmental sources, and such information from non-governmental sources as may be of interest to the Agency.

6. In the performance of their duties, the General Secretary and the staff shall not seek or receive instructions from any Government or from any other authority external to the Agency and shall refrain from any action which might reflect on their position as international officials responsible only to the Agency; subject to their responsibility to the Agency, they shall not disclose any industrial secrets or other confidential information coming to their knowledge by reason of their official duties in the Agency.

7. Each of the Contracting Parties undertakes to respect the exclusively international character of the responsibilities of the General Secretary and the staff and not to seek to influence them in the discharge of their responsibilities.

Control system

ARTICLE 12

1. For the purpose of verifying compliance with the obligations entered into by the Contracting Parties in accordance with article 1, a control system shall be established which shall be put into effect in accordance with the provisions of articles 13–18 of this Treaty.

2. The control system shall be used in particular for the purpose of verifying:

(a) That devices, services and facilities intended for peaceful uses of nuclear energy are not used in the testing or manufacture of nuclear weapons;

(b) That none of the activities prohibited in article 1 of this Treaty are carried out in the territory of the Contracting Parties with nuclear materials or weapons introduced from abroad, and

(c) That explosions for peaceful purposes are compatible with article 18 of this Treaty.

IAEA safeguards

ARTICLE 13

Each Contracting Party shall negotiate multilateral or bilateral agreements with the International Atomic Energy Agency for the application of its safeguards to its nuclear activities. Each Contracting Party shall initiate negotiations within a period of 180 days after the date of the deposit of its instrument of ratification of this Treaty. These agreements shall enter into force, for each Party, not later than eighteen months after the date of the initiation of such negotiations except in case of unforeseen circumstances or *force majeure*.

Reports of the parties

ARTICLE 14

1. The Contracting Parties shall submit to the Agency and to the International Atomic Energy Agency, for their information, semi-annual reports stating that no activity prohibited under this Treaty has occurred in their respective territories.

2. The Contracting Parties shall simultaneously transmit to the

Agency a copy of any report they may submit to the International Atomic Energy Agency which relates to matters that are the subject of this Treaty and to the application of safeguards.

3. The Contracting Parties shall also transmit to the Organization of American States, for its information, any reports that may be of interest to it, in accordance with the obligations established by the Inter-American System.

Special reports requested by the General Secretary

ARTICLE 15

1. With the authorization of the Council, the General Secretary may request any of the Contracting Parties to provide the Agency with complementary or supplementary information regarding any event or circumstance connected with compliance with this Treaty, explaining his reasons. The Contracting Parties undertake to co-operate promptly and fully with the General Secretary.

2. The General Secretary shall inform the Council and the Contracting Parties forthwith of such requests and of the respective replies.

Special inspections

ARTICLE 16

1. The International Atomic Energy Agency and the Council established by this Treaty have the power of carrying out special inspections in the following cases:

(a) In the case of the International Atomic Energy Agency, in accordance with the agreements referred to in article 13 of the Treaty;

(b) In the case of the Council:

(i) When so requested, the reasons for the request being stated, by any Party which suspects that some activity prohibited by this Treaty has been carried out or is about to be carried out, either in the territory of any other Party or in any other place on such latter Party's behalf, the Council shall immediately arrange for such an inspection in accordance with article 10, paragraph 5.

(ii) When requested by any Party which has been suspected of or charged with having violated the Treaty, the Council shall immediately arrange for the special inspection requested, in accordance with article 10, paragraph 5.

The above requests will be made to the Council through the General Secretary.

2.   The costs and expenses of any special inspection carried out under paragraph 1, sub-paragraph (*b*), sections (i) and (ii) of this article shall be borne by the requesting Party or Parties, except where the Council concludes on the basis of the report on the special inspection that, in view of the circumstances existing in the case, such costs and expenses should be borne by the Agency.

3.   The General Conference shall formulate the procedures for the organization and execution of the special inspections carried out in accordance with paragraph 1, sub-paragraph (*b*), sections (i) and (ii) of this article.

4.   The Contracting Parties undertake to grant the inspectors carrying out such special inspections full and free access to all places and all information which may be necessary for the performance of their duties and which are directly and intimately connected with the suspicion of violation of this Treaty. If so requested by the Contracting Party in whose territory the inspection is carried out, the inspectors designated by the General Conference shall be accompanied by representatives of the authorities of that Contracting Party, provided that this does not in any way delay or hinder the work of the inspectors.

5.   The Council shall immediately transmit to all the Parties, through the General Secretary, a copy of any report resulting from special inspections.

6.   Similarly, the Council shall send through the General Secretary to the Secretary-General of the United Nations for transmission to the United Nations Security Council and General Assembly, and to the Council of the Organization of American States for its information, a copy of any report resulting from any special inspection carried out in accordance with paragraph 1, sub-paragraph (*b*), sections (i) and (ii) of this article.

7.   The Council may decide, or any Contracting Party may request, the convening of a special session of the General Conference for the purpose of considering the reports resulting from any special inspection. In such a case, the General Secretary shall take immediate steps to convene the special session requested.

8.   The General Conference, convened in special session under this article, may make recommendations to the Contracting Parties and submit reports to the Secretary-General of the United Nations to be transmitted to the Security Council and the General Assembly.

Use of nuclear energy for peaceful purposes

ARTICLE 17

Nothing in the provisions of this Treaty shall prejudice the rights of the Contracting Parties, in conformity with this Treaty, to use nuclear energy for peaceful purposes, in particular for their economic development and social progress.

Explosions for peaceful purposes

ARTICLE 18

1. The Contracting Parties may carry out explosions of nuclear devices for peaceful purposes—including explosions which involve devices similar to those used in nuclear weapons—or collaborate with third parties for the same purpose, provided that they do so in accordance with the provisions of this article and the other articles of the Treaty, particularly articles 1 and 5.

2. Contracting Parties intending to carry out, or co-operate in the carrying out of such, an explosion shall notify the Agency and the International Atomic Energy Agency, as far in advance as the circumstances require, of the date of the explosion and shall at the same time provide the following information:

(a) The nature of the nuclear device and the source from which it was obtained;

(b) The place and purpose of the planned explosion;

(c) The procedures which will be followed in order to comply with paragraph 3 of this article;

(d) The expected force of the device;

(e) The fullest possible information on any possible radioactive fall-out that may result from the explosion or explosions, and the measures which will be taken to avoid danger to the population, flora and fauna, and territories of any other Party or Parties.

3. The General Secretary and the technical personnel designated by the Council and the International Atomic Energy Agency may observe all the preparations, including the explosion of the device, and shall have unrestricted access to any area in the vicinity of the site of the explosion in order to ascertain whether the device and the procedures followed during the explosion are in conformity with the in-

formation supplied under paragraph 2 of the present article and the other provisions of this Treaty.

4.   The Contracting Parties may accept the collaboration of third parties for the purpose set forth in paragraph 1 of the present article, in accordance with paragraphs 2 and 3 thereof.

Relations with other international organizations

ARTICLE 19

1.   The Agency may conclude such agreements with the International Atomic Energy Agency as are authorized by the General Conference and as it considers likely to facilitate the efficient operation of the control system established by this Treaty.

2.   The Agency may also enter into relations with any international organization or body, especially any which may be established in the future to supervise disarmament or measures for the control of armaments in any part of the world.

3.   The Contracting Parties may, if they see fit, request the advice of the Inter-American Nuclear Energy Commission on all technical matters connected with the application of the Treaty with which the Commission is competent to deal under its Statute.

Measures in the event of violation of the Treaty

ARTICLE 20

1.   The General Conference shall take note of all cases in which, in its opinion, any Contracting Party is not complying fully with its obligations under this Treaty and shall draw the matter to the attention of the Party concerned, making such recommendations as it deems appropriate.

2.   If, in its opinion, such non-compliance constitutes a violation of this Treaty which might endanger peace and security, the General Conference shall report thereon simultaneously to the Security Council and the General Assembly through the Secretary-General of the United Nations and to the Council of the Organization of American States. The General Conference shall likewise report to the International Atomic Energy Agency for such purposes as are relevant in accordance with its Statute.

United Nations and Organization of American States

ARTICLE 21

None of the provisions of this Treaty shall be construed as impairing the rights and obligations of the Parties under the Charter of the United Nations or, in the case of States members of the Organization of American States, under existing regional treaties.

Privileges and immunities

ARTICLE 22

1. The Agency shall enjoy in the territory of each of the Contracting Parties such legal capacity and such privileges and immunities as may be necessary for the exercise of its functions and the fulfilment of its purposes.

2. Representatives of the Contracting Parties accredited to the Agency and officials of the Agency shall similarly enjoy such privileges and immunities as are necessary for the performance of their functions.

3. The Agency may conclude agreements with the Contracting Parties with a view to determining the details of the application of paragraphs 1 and 2 of this article.

Notification of other agreements

ARTICLE 23

Once this Treaty has entered into force, the Secretariat shall be notified immediately of any international agreement concluded by any of the Contracting Parties on matters with which this Treaty is concerned; the Secretariat shall register it and notify the other Contracting Parties.

Settlement of disputes

ARTICLE 24

Unless the Parties concerned agree on another mode of peaceful settlement, any question or dispute concerning the interpretation or application of this Treaty which is not settled shall be referred to the International Court of Justice with the prior consent of the parties to the controversy.

Signature

ARTICLE 25

1.   This Treaty shall be open indefinitely for signature by:

(*a*)   All the Latin American Republics;

(*b*)   All other sovereign States situated in their entirety south of latitude 35° north in the western hemisphere; and, except as provided in paragraph 2 of this article, all such States which become sovereign, when they have been admitted by the General Conference.

2.   The General Conference shall not take any decision regarding the admission of a political entity part or all of whose territory is the subject, prior to the date when this Treaty is opened for signature, of a dispute or claim between an extra-continental country and one or more Latin American States, so long as the dispute has not been settled by peaceful means.

Ratification and deposit

ARTICLE 26

1.   This Treaty shall be subject to ratification by signatory States in accordance with their respective constitutional procedures.

2.   This Treaty and the instruments of ratification shall be deposited with the Government of the United States of Mexico, which is hereby designated the Depositary Government.

3.   The Depositary Government shall send certified copies of this Treaty to the Governments of signatory States and shall notify them of the deposit of each instrument of ratification.

Reservations

ARTICLE 27

This Treaty shall not be subject to reservations.

Entry into force

ARTICLE 28

1.   Subject to the provisions of paragraphs 2 and 3 of this article, this Treaty shall enter into force among the States that have ratified it as soon as the following requirements have been met:

(*a*) Deposit of the instruments of ratification of this Treaty with the Depositary Government by the Governments of the States mentioned in article 25 which are in existence on the date when this Treaty is opened for signature and which are not affected by the provisions of article 25, paragraph 2;

(*b*) Signature and ratification of Additional Protocol I annexed to this Treaty by all extra-continental and continental States having *de jure* or *de facto* international responsibility for territories situated in the zone of application of the Treaty;

(*c*) Signature and ratification of the Additional Protocol II annexed to this Treaty by all powers possessing nuclear weapons;

(*d*) Conclusion of bilateral agreements on the application of the Safeguards System of the International Atomic Energy Agency in accordance with article 13 of this Treaty.

2. All signatory States shall have the imprescriptible right to waive, wholly or in part, the requirements laid down in the preceding paragraph. They may do so by means of a declaration which shall be annexed to their respective instruments of ratification and which may be formulated at the time of deposit of the instrument or subsequently. For those States which exercise this right, this Treaty shall enter into force upon deposit of the declaration, or as soon as those requirements have been met which have not been expressly waived.

3. As soon as this Treaty has entered into force in accordance with the provisions of paragraph 2 for eleven States, the Depositary Government shall convene a preliminary meeting of those States in order that the Agency may be set up and commence its work.

4. After the entry into force of the Treaty for all the countries of the zone, the rise of a new power possessing nuclear weapons shall have the effect of suspending the execution of this Treaty for those countries which have ratified it without waiving the requirements of paragraph 1, sub-paragraph (*c*) of this article, and which request such suspension; the Treaty shall remain suspended until the new power, on its own initiative or upon request by the General Conference, ratifies the annexed Additional Protocol II.

Amendments

ARTICLE 29

1. Any Contracting Party may propose amendments to this Treaty and shall submit their proposals to the Council through the General

Secretary, who shall transmit them to all the other Contracting Parties and, in addition, to signatories in accordance with article 6. The Council, through the General Secretary, shall, immediately following the meeting of signatories, convene a special session of the General Conference to examine the proposals made, for the adoption of which a two-thirds majority of the Contracting Parties present and voting shall be required.

2.   Amendments adopted shall enter into force as soon as the requirements set forth in article 28 of this Treaty have been complied with.

Duration and denunciation

ARTICLE 30

1.   This Treaty shall be of a permanent nature and shall remain in force indefinitely, but any Party may denounce it by notifying the General Secretary of the Agency if, in the opinion of the denouncing State, there have arisen or may arise circumstances connected with the content of the Treaty or of the annexed Additional Protocols I and II which affect its supreme interests and the peace and security of one or more Contracting Parties.

2.   The denunciation shall take effect three months after the delivery to the General Secretary of the Agency of the notification by the Government of the signatory State concerned. The General Secretary shall immediately communicate such notification to the other Contracting Parties and to the Secretary-General of the United Nations for the information of the Security Council and the General Assembly of the United Nations. He shall also communicate it to the Secretary General of the Organization of American States.

Authentic texts and registration

ARTICLE 31

This Treaty, of which the Spanish, Chinese, English, French, Portuguese and Russian texts are equally authentic, shall be registered by the Depositary Government in accordance with Article 102 of the United Nations Charter. The Depositary Government shall notify the Secretary-General of the United Nations of the signatures, ratifications and amendments relating to this Treaty and shall communicate them to the

Secretary General of the Organization of American States for his information.

TRANSITIONAL ARTICLE

Denunciation of the declaration referred to in article 28, paragraph 2, shall be subject to the same procedures as the denunciation of the Treaty, except that it shall take effect on the date of delivery of the respective notification.

IN WITNESS WHEREOF the undersigned Plenipotentiaries, having deposited their full powers, found in good and due form, sign this Treaty on behalf of their respective Governments.

DONE at Mexico City, Distrito Federal, on the fourteenth day of February, one thousand nine hundred and sixty-seven.

Additional Protocol I

The undersigned Plenipotentiaries, furnished with full powers by their respective Governments,

Convinced that the Treaty for the Prohibition of Nuclear Weapons in Latin America, negotiated and signed in accordance with the recommendations of the General Assembly of the United Nations in resolution 1911 (XVIII) of 27 November 1963, represents an important step towards ensuring the non-proliferation of nuclear weapons,

Aware that the non-proliferation of nuclear weapons is not an end in itself but rather a means of achieving general and complete disarmament at a later stage,

Desiring to contribute, so far as lies in their power, towards ending the armaments race, especially in the field of nuclear weapons, and towards strengthening a world at peace, based on mutual respect and sovereign equality of States,

Have agreed as follows:

ARTICLE 1

To undertake to apply the status of denuclearization in respect of warlike purposes as defined in articles 1, 3, 5 and 13 of the Treaty for the Prohibition of Nuclear Weapons in Latin America in territories for which, *de jure* or *de facto*, they are internationally responsible and which lie within the limits of the geographical zone established in that Treaty.

ARTICLE 2

The duration of this Protocol shall be the same as that of the Treaty for the Prohibition of Nuclear Weapons in Latin America of which this Protocol is an annex, and the provisions regarding ratification and denunciation contained in the Treaty shall be applicable to it.

ARTICLE 3

This Protocol shall enter into force, for the States which have ratified it, on the date of the deposit of their respective instruments of ratification.

IN WITNESS WHEREOF the undersigned Plenipotentiaries, having deposited their full powers, found in good and due form, sign this Treaty on behalf of their respective Governments.

Additional Protocol II

The undersigned Plenipotentiaries, furnished with full powers by their respective Governments,

Convinced that the Treaty for the Prohibition of Nuclear Weapons in Latin America, negotiated and signed in accordance with the recommendations of the General Assembly of the United Nations in resolution 1911 (XVIII) of 27 November 1963, is an important step towards ensuring the non-proliferation of nuclear weapons,

Aware that the non-proliferation of nuclear weapons is not an end in itself but rather a means for achieving general and complete disarmament at a later stage,

Desiring to contribute, so far as lies in their power, towards ending the armaments race, especially in the field of nuclear weapons, and towards promoting and strengthening a world at peace based on mutual respect and sovereign equality of States,

Have agreed as follows:

ARTICLE 1

The status of denuclearization of Latin America in respect of warlike purposes, as defined, delimited and set forth in the Treaty for the Prohibition of Nuclear Weapons in Latin America of which this instrument is an annex, shall be fully respected by the Parties to this Protocol in all its express aims and provisions.

ARTICLE 2

The Governments represented by the undersigned Plenipotentiaries undertake, therefore, not to contribute in any way to the performance of acts involving a violation of the obligations of article 1 of the Treaty in the territories to which the Treaty applies in accordance with article 4 thereof.

ARTICLE 3

The Governments represented by the undersigned Plenipotentiaries also undertake not to use or threaten to use nuclear weapons against the Contracting Parties of the Treaty for the Prohibition of Nuclear Weapons in Latin America.

ARTICLE 4

The duration of this Protocol shall be the same as that of the Treaty for the Prohibition of Nuclear Weapons in Latin America of which this Protocol is an annex, and the definitions of territory and nuclear weapons set forth in articles 3 and 5 of the Treaty shall be applicable to the Protocol, as well as the provisions regarding ratification, reservations, denunciation, authentic texts and registration contained in articles 26, 27, 30 and 31 of the Treaty.

ARTICLE 5

This Protocol shall enter into force, for the States which have ratified it, on the date of the deposit of their respective instruments of ratification.

IN WITNESS WHEREOF the undersigned Plenipotentiaries, having deposited their full powers, found in good and due form, sign this Treaty on behalf of their respective Governments.

Appendix III

Treaty Banning Nuclear Weapon Tests in the Atmosphere,
in Outer Space and Under Water
Signed at Moscow on 5 August 1963 by the USSR,
the United Kingdom and the United States

The Governments of the United States of America, the United Kingdom of Great Britain and Northern Ireland, and the Union of Soviet Socialist Republics, hereinafter referred to as the "Original Parties,"

Proclaiming as their principal aim the speediest possible achievement of an agreement on general and complete disarmament under strict international control in accordance with the objectives of the United Nations which would put an end to the armaments race and eliminate the incentive to the production and testing of all kinds of weapons, including nuclear weapons,

Seeking to achieve the discontinuance of all test explosions of nuclear weapons for all time, determined to continue negotiations to this end, and desiring to put an end to the contamination of man's environment by radioactive substances,

Have agreed as follows:

ARTICLE I

1. Each of the Parties to this Treaty undertakes to prohibit, to prevent, and not to carry out any nuclear weapon test explosion, or any other nuclear explosion, at any place under its jurisdiction or control:

(*a*) in the atmosphere; beyond its limits, including outer space; or under water, including territorial waters or high seas; or

(*b*) in any other environment if such explosion causes radioactive debris to be present outside the territorial limits of the State under whose jurisdiction or control such explosion is conducted. It is understood in this connection that the provisions of this subparagraph are without prejudice to the conclusion of a treaty resulting in the permanent banning of all nuclear test explosions, including all such explosions underground, the conclusion of which, as the Parties have stated in the Preamble to this Treaty, they seek to achieve.

2. Each of the Parties to this Treaty undertakes furthermore to refrain from causing, encouraging, or in any way participating in, the carrying out of any nuclear weapon test explosion, or any other nuclear explosion, anywhere which would take place in any of the environments described, or have the effect referred to, in paragraph 1 of this Article.

ARTICLE II

1. Any Party may propose amendments to this Treaty. The text of any proposed amendment shall be submitted to the Depositary Governments which shall circulate it to all Parties to this Treaty. Thereafter, if requested to do so by one-third or more of the Parties, the Depositary Governments shall convene a conference, to which they shall invite all the Parties, to consider such amendment.

2. Any amendment to this Treaty must be approved by a majority of the votes of all the Parties to this Treaty, including the votes of all of the Original Parties. The amendment shall enter into force for all Parties upon the deposit of instruments of ratification by a majority of all the Parties, including the instruments of ratification of all of the Original Parties.

ARTICLE III

1. This Treaty shall be open to all States for signature. Any State which does not sign this Treaty before its entry into force in accordance with paragraph 3 of this Article may accede to it at any time.

2. This Treaty shall be subject to ratification by signatory States. Instruments of ratification and instruments of accession shall be deposited with the Governments of the Original Parties—the United States of America, the United Kingdom of Great Britain and Northern Ireland, and the Union of Soviet Socialist Republics—which are hereby designated the Depositary Governments.

3. This treaty shall enter into force after its ratification by all the Original Parties and the deposit of their instruments of ratification.

4. For States whose instruments of ratification or accession are deposited subsequent to the entry into force of this Treaty, it shall enter into force on the date of the deposit of their instruments of ratification or accession.

5. The Depositary Governments shall promptly inform all signatory

and acceding States of the date of each signature, the date of deposit of each instrument of ratification of and accession to this Treaty, the date of its entry into force, and the date of receipt of any requests for conferences or other notices.

6.   This Treaty shall be registered by the Depositary Governments pursuant to Article 102 of the Charter of the United Nations.

ARTICLE IV

This Treaty shall be of unlimited duration.

Each Party shall in exercising its national sovereignty have the right to withdraw from the Treaty if it decides that extraordinary events, related to the subject matter of this Treaty, have jeopardized the supreme interests of its country. It shall give notice of such withdrawal to all other Parties to the Treaty three months in advance.

ARTICLE V

This Treaty, of which the English and Russian texts are equally authentic, shall be deposited in the archives of the Depositary Governments. Duly certified copies of this Treaty shall be transmitted by the Depositary Governments to the Governments of the signatory and acceding States.

IN WITNESS WHEREOF the undersigned, duly authorized, have signed this Treaty.

DONE in triplicate at the city of Moscow the fifth day of August, one thousand nine hundred and sixty-three.

Bibliography

Frequently used short titles or abbreviations are given in brackets following the story.

I. Documents

Dulles Papers, John Foster Dulles Library, Princeton, N.J.

Eighteen-Nation Committee on Disarmament. *Verbatim Records.* 1962–1967. [ENDC/PV.]

Scott, James Brown (ed.), *Proceeding of the Hague Peace Conferences: The Conference of 1899*, Oxford University Press, 1920.

United Nations. General Assembly. *Relevant Documents & Summary Records.* [A and A/SR]

United Nations. Security Council. *Relevant Documents & Summary Records.* [SC and SC/SR]

United Nations, *The United Nations and Disarmament*, United Nations, Office of Public Information, New York, 1967.

United States Atomic Energy Commission. *In the Matter of J. Robert Oppenheimer*, Transcript of the Hearings before the Personnel Security Board, April 12, 1954–May 6, 1954.

United States Atomic Energy Commission. *Annual Report to Congress—1963*, Washington, GPO, 1964.

U.S. Arms Control and Disarmament Agency, *Documents on Disarmament, 1962–1967.*

U.S. Arms Control and Disarmament Agency, "To Prevent the Spread of Nuclear Weapons," Publication 26, September 1965.

U.S. Congress. *Committee on Foreign Relations*, "Nominations of Robert R. Bowie and U. Alexis Johnson." August 16 and 23, 1966, Committee on Foreign Relations, Washington, 1966.

U.S. Congress. *Hearings: Nuclear Test Ban Treaty*, 88th Congress, 1st Session, GPO, 1963.

U.S. Congress. *Joint Committee on Atomic Energy. AEC Authorizing Legislation for Fiscal Year 1965*, Part I, GPO, 1964.

U.S. Congress. *Joint Committee on Atomic Energy. Hearings: Amending* the *Atomic Energy Act of 1954*. 85th Congress, 2nd Session, GPO, 1958.

U.S. Department of State, *A Report on the International Control of Atomic Energy (The Acheson-Lilienthal Report)*. Publication 2498, Washington, 1946.

II. Books

Aron, Raymond. *The Great Debate: Theories of Nuclear Strategy*. Doubleday, New York, 1965.

Beaton, Leonard. *Must the Bomb Spread?* Penguin Books, Harmondswerth, England, 1966.

Beaton, Leonard and Maddox, John. *The Spread of Nuclear Weapons*. Chatto and Windus, London, 1962.

Bechhoefer, Bernhard. *Postwar Negotiations for Arms Control*. The Brookings Institute, Washington, D.C., 1961.

Bennett, John C. (ed.). *Nuclear Weapons and Conflict of Conscience*. Scribner, New York, 1962.

Buchan, Alastair (ed.). *A World of Nuclear Powers?* Columbia University, Prentice-Hall, New York, 1966.

Chakravarti, P. C. *India's China Policy*. Indiana University Press, Bloomington, 1962.

Churchill, Randolph S. (ed.). *Europe Unite: Speeches in 1947 and 1948 by Winston S. Churchill*. Houghton Mifflin, Boston, 1950.

Davidson, William C., Kalkstein, Marvin I., Hohenemser, Christoph. *The Nth Country Problem and Arms Control*. National Planning Association, Washington, 1960.

Dean, Gordon. *Report on the Atom*. Knopf, New York, 1953.

Duynstee, A. E. M. (ed.). *Nuclear Weapons*. Western European Union Assembly, Committee on Defense Questions and Armaments, 1964.

Jacobson, Harold K. and Stein, Eric. *Diplomats, Scientists, and Politicians: The United States and the Nuclear Test Ban Negotiations*. University of Michigan Press, Ann Arbor, 1966.

Kramish, Arnold. *The Peaceful Atom in Foreign Policy*. Harper and Row, New York, 1963.

Maruyama, Masao. *Thought and Behaviour in Modern Japanese Politics*. Oxford University Press, London, 1963.

Mendel, Douglas H. *The Japanese People and Foreign Policy*. University of California Press, Berkeley, 1961.

Morriss, Ivan I. *Nationalism and the Right Wing in Japan*. Oxford University Press, London, 1960.

Nagle, William J. *Morality and Modern Warfare, The State of the Question.* Helicon Press, Baltimore, 1960.

Rosecrance, R. N. (ed.). *The Dispersion of Nuclear Weapons.* Columbia University Press, New York, 1964.

Schlesinger, Arthur M., Jr. *A Thousand Days: John F. Kennedy in the White House.* Houghton Mifflin Co., Boston, 1965.

Sorenson, Theodore C. *Kennedy.* Harper and Row, New York, 1965.

III. Newspapers and Periodicals

Atomic News Digest
Bulletin of the Atomic Scientists
Christian Science Monitor
India News
Indian and Foreign Review
The Israel Digest
Japan Times Weekly
Jewish Observer and Middle East Review
London Times
The New York Times
Nucleonics
The Observer
Overseas Hindustan Times
United States Department of State Bulletin

IV. Articles

"The Bomb." *Seminar.* January, 1965.

Halle, Louis J. "Any Number Can Play Nuclear Chicken." *New York Times Magazine.* November 8, 1964.

Levi, Werner. "Indian Neutralism Reconsidered." *Pacific Affairs.* XXXVIII, No. 2 (Summer 1964).

Miksche, F. O. "The Expansion of the Atomic Club." *Survival.* London, September–October, 1960.

Peres, Shimon. "Problems of Israel's Security." *Israel Year Book.* 1963.

Smith, R. E. "Three Possible Engineering Applications of Nuclear Explosives in the Shale Oil Industry." Sandia Corporation. SC-RR-65-657, October 1966.

Tucker, Robert W. *Stability and the Nth Country Problem.* Study Memorandum, *Institute for Defense Analyses.* Washington, D.C., November 1961.

Weiner, Myron. "Whither India? Unity and Diversity." *Asia*. No. 3 (Spring, 1965).

Witherspoon, Paul A. "Economics of Nuclear Explosives in Developing Underground Gas Storage." Lawrence Radiation Laboratory, University of California at Livermore. UCRL-14877 of July 29, 1966.

Wohlstetter, Albert. "Nuclear Sharing: NATO and the Nth Country." *Foreign Affairs*. April, 1961.

Index